DATE DUE

MA. 05.1999			
APR.20.1999			
APR 20			
			Printed in USA

HIGHSMITH #45230

the Accelerated Reader

Computerized Reading Management Program ™

Grade Level

Book Number

Points

Ranald Slidell Mackenzie

Brave Cavalry Colonel

Ranald S. Mackenzie, United States Military Academy, 1862.
— Photo courtesy United States Military Academy Archives

Ranald Slidell Mackenzie

Brave Cavalry Colonel

By J'Nell L. Pate

J'Nell L. Pate

EAKIN PRESS ★ AUSTIN, TEXAS

FIRST EDITION

Copyright © 1994
By J'Nell L. Pate

Published in the United States of America
By Eakin Press
An Imprint of Sunbelt Media, Inc.
P.O. Drawer 90159 ★ Austin, TX 78709-0159

ISBN 0-89015-901-7

T.H. JOHNSON
ELEMENTARY

63036

Library of Congress Cataloging-in-Publication Data

Pate, J'Nell L.
    Ranald Slidell Mackenzie : brave cavalry colonel / by J'Nell L. Pate.
        p. cm.
    Includes index.
    Summary: Traces the life and military career of the 1862 West Point
graduate who spent much of his life as a cavalry officer fighting the
Indians in Texas.
    ISBN 0-89015-901-7 : $14.95
    1. Mackenzie, Ranald Slidell, 1840–1889 — Juvenile literature. 2.
Indians of North America — Wars — 1866–1895 — Juvenile literature.
3. Generals — Texas — Biography — Juvenile literature. 4. United
States. Army. Cavalry, 4th — History — 19th century — Juvenile
literature. 5. Frontier and pioneer life — Texas — Juvenile literature.
6. Texas — History — 1846–1950 — Juvenile literature. [1. Mackenzie,
Ranald Slidell, 1840–1889. 2. Generals. 3. Indians of North America —
Wars — 1866–1895. 4. United States. Army. Cavalry, 4th — History.
5. Texas — History — 1846–1950.] I. Title.
E83.866.M33P37   1993
355'.0092--dc20
[B]   93-21952
                                                               CIP
                                                                AC

To Kenneth

Contents

Ranald Slidell Mackenzie, age twenty-four.
— Photo courtesy National Archives, 111-B-2735

Part I

Early Years: 1840–1869

1

Chapter One

A Career for Ranald

C ertainly a young man with the long, impressive name of Ranald Slidell Mackenzie had a prominent family background which in part explained why he was named that. His grandmother, the only child of a prominent Scottish family living in New York, had married a poor candlemaker named John Slidell soon after the close of the Revolutionary War. The two had raised a huge family of Slidells who began to make their mark on the early nineteenth-century United States. One of their sons, Alexander, would later become Ranald's father.

Reserved, serious-minded Alexander Slidell appeared overshadowed by his older brother John. If anyone possessed the ability to raise the name Slidell to prominence in the United States, his brother John certainly did. So, in 1838, out of respect to his mother's family, Alexander added his mother's maiden name of Mackenzie to his own. He became Alexander Slidell Mackenzie.

As a career officer in the United States Navy, Alexander took advantage of the solitude of his many months at sea and began writing books. His biography of Commodore Oliver Hazard Perry, who won a battle in

2

Lake Erie during the War of 1812, became popular. Oliver and his younger brother, Matthew Calbraith Perry, visited the Slidell family often. Another of Alexander's books told of John Paul Jones, who had made a name for himself in the Revolutionary War. Alexander liked naval heroes.

Alexander soon took a wife, Catherine Robinson, and their first child, a daughter, they named Harriet. Finally, at the family home in New York City, the son they wanted to perpetuate the name of Mackenzie appeared on July 27, 1840. His parents decided to name him Ranald Slidell Mackenzie. A few weeks later, the family of four moved to a farm on the Hudson River between Tarrytown and Ossining.

A Navy father cannot forever remain with his family. Alexander Mackenzie became a commander in 1841 and continued his sea voyages. The quiet young officer maintained a reserve that kept him apart from his subordinates. Exacting with himself, he upheld a rigid discipline on his ship. Ranald would inherit some of these same traits from his father.

The next year Alexander's assignment took him on a training ship, the *Somers,* for young naval officers. The ship sailed to the African coast and back to the United States on its training mission. On the return voyage, Commander Mackenzie discovered that a possible mutiny threatened his life and those of his ship's officers, and he arrested three ringleaders. Fearing that the sympathizers would release the captives and instigate their rebellion, Alexander saw no solution to the problem but to execute the three guilty young men. Unfortunately for his later career, one of the three mutinous young men happened to be Philip Spencer, the son of Secretary of War John Spencer. Never one to shirk what he felt to be his duty, Alexander Mackenzie carried through with the shipboard hanging. Naturally, when Commander Mackenzie's ship docked in New York, the secretary of war court-martialed him. The inquiry cleared Mackenzie of any wrongdoing because the secretary's son had a long reputation as a troublemaker, but Alexander's promising naval career failed to progress after the incident.

Further problems troubled the commander. His young son Ranald had suffered a sunstroke at age three, causing the child to be frail. Alexander and his wife feared that Ranald would be in ill health most of his life. However, two other sons soon arrived to brighten the commander's sad life — Alexander Slidell Mackenzie, Jr., and Morris Robinson Slidell Mackenzie.

In 1846 the commander left his family once more to fight in the Mexican War. Two years later, when Ranald was only eight, Alexander Mackenzie died of a heart attack. His family always blamed the humiliation of the court-martial for the deterioration in health that eventually led to the commander's early death.

Ranald's mother soon sold the farm and moved her small family to Morristown, New Jersey, to be nearer her own relatives. Despite his frailty as a child, Ranald earned the respect of the other boys of Morristown for his courage and fine character. He seemed compelled to prove himself before his friends to make up for his father's reputation. Though his schoolmates might whisper about the unfortunate turn of events in the older Mackenzie's career, they could only respect the remainder of Ranald's family.

Ranald's Slidell aunts and uncles brought honor to their name. Aunt Jane Slidell married Commodore Matthew C. Perry, who opened Japan for trade with the western world in 1853. By this time two Slidell uncles, John and Tom, held prominent positions in Louisiana political affairs. John served as United States senator from that state, while Tom performed the duties of chief justice of the Louisiana Supreme Court. Then Ranald's first cousin, Caroline Perry, daughter of Jane and Matthew Perry, married August Belmont, the United States representative of a famous European banking family, the Rothschilds. Caroline was probably one of the wealthiest young women in the country.

In the autumn of 1855, when Ranald was fifteen, he entered Williams College at Williamstown, Massachusetts. An uncle suggested that he prepare himself for the study of law. A classmate of Ranald's at Williams later described him: "Very quiet, modest to shyness, and with a little lisp, Ranald was a good fellow; we all loved him and were both sorry and proud when the appointment [to West Point] came to him ... but we did not ... forecast his future; he had not at that time given any indications of the kind of character he was to develop."

Two years later, in the spring of 1857, the still slender sixteen-year-old Ranald Mackenzie sat in his room at Williams College. He really did not like the study of law. He knew that his grades weren't anything to brag about. He liked school well enough and got along well with the young men in Kappa Alpha fraternity, spending a great deal of time with them, even though he still retained his boyhood shyness. But was law the career that would make the name Mackenzie as prominent and respected as it should be? Ranald had decided that it was not.

He had an idea that he planned to spring on his mother and any uncles who happened to be around giving advice the next time he was home. Wouldn't he be more likely to make a name for himself as a general in the United States Army than as a lawyer or even a politician? The prospect cheered him.

A year later, young Ranald seemed further on his way toward an Army career. At the Williams College Junior Rhetorical Exhibition, on June 1, 1858, Ranald spoke on military tactics. That seemed a little more practical than the topics his classmates chose, such as the Druids, intellectual homage, and Ignatius Loyola.

Through the assistance of his congressman from the state of New Jersey, Ranald received an appointment to the military academy at West Point. Despite the fears expressed by his family that his weak physical frame could not stand up to a military life, Ranald would enter the academy, and an Army career would at last be his.

Ranald's younger brother, Alexander, their father's namesake, had already left home to join the Navy. The two young men no doubt felt that they owed it to their father's memory to make successful military careers and further distinguish the Mackenzie name that their father had adopted.

Chapter Two

West Point Cadet

West Point fulfilled many of the dreams Ranald had envisioned about it. For the first time, he really became interested in his studies. The reports sent home recorded his growing success, to the surprise of his family and friends. At the end of his first year the popular Ranald ranked fifth in his class scholastically. By the close of his second year, in 1860, he rose to second in his class.

Catherine Mackenzie humorously wrote her son of the surprise among family and friends concerning his accomplishments. She told him that their preacher told her, "No, it is not possible; madam, I had ventured to hint to my wife in strict confidence my certainty of the disappointment in store for you."

Ranald's junior year at West Point became confused somewhat by the general excitement following the outbreak of the Civil War in April 1861. Many of his classmates dropped out of school to volunteer their services to the rebellious South. A very sensitive person, Ranald naturally became upset by the situation. It meant that his own family would be divided. His two uncles who had chosen Louisiana as their home would support the

South. Uncle John Slidell had been an important man in the Senate and even a diplomat to Mexico in 1845, so he probably would accept an equally important position with the new government that was being formed in Montgomery, Alabama.

When college officials tabulated rank positions in June 1862, Ranald had dropped to twelfth. This placed him nearly in the middle of his small class.

A young man whom Mackenzie knew at West Point, George Armstrong Custer, became involved in various scrapes upon many occasions. Fellow cadets saw him quite often on the parade ground, walking off demerits. One year older than Ranald, George surprised many who knew him at the Point in that he managed to graduate at all. Out of thirty-four, he ranked last in his class upon graduation that year of the outbreak of the war. He went right into the fighting and soon distinguished himself because of his bold nature.

In the fall of 1861, Ranald's senior year, another incident burst upon the international scene. The Confederacy decided to send two of their dependable statesmen to Europe to seek aid. One would go to Great Britain, the other to France. The men made it through the blockade and safely reached Havana, Cuba. There they boarded a British ship, the *Trent,* en route to the British Isles. A Northern ship, the *San Jacinto,* captained by Charles Wilkes, stopped the *Trent* and seized the two Southern diplomats — James Mason and John Slidell. Ironically, Captain Wilkes and Ranald's Uncle John had once spent a great deal of time together as boyhood friends. Their association had ended in a jealous brawl over an actress many years before the *Trent* affair.

If someone had conducted a poll in the early months of 1862 to determine the two most hated men in the North, Ranald's Uncle John and James Mason would have won with no trouble. The British government demanded that the United States apologize for stopping the *Trent* and removing the two passengers. The two nations were almost on the verge of war because of the incident.

In January 1862, the United States government finally released Mason and Slidell, and they resumed their voyage to Europe. While Mason traveled to England, it became Slidell's assignment to persuade the king of France to aid the South.

During his senior year at West Point, Ranald served as an assistant professor of mathematics. Upon graduation on June 17, 1862, he ranked first in his class of twenty-eight.

As he stood with his class at the close of the graduation ceremony, holding his diploma and his commission as a second lieutenant in the United States Army, Ranald was ready to fight for the North in the Civil War. He wondered what his orders would be.

Chapter Three

A Gallant Soldier

T he slender young Ranald Slidell Mackenzie, at twenty-one a second lieutenant in the United States Army, read his orders. He had been made second lieutenant of engineers and was assigned to Gen. Ambrose E. Burnsides' corps of the Army of the Potomac, which held orders to move from Washington toward Richmond. Along the route, engineers were to bridge numerous streams ahead of the advancing troops. This became Mackenzie's assignment: "Prepare locations for and construct pontoon bridges. Also select at banks and fords good positions for batteries to cover crossings at these places, in the woods, if possible."

Mackenzie reported for active duty and did his best to carry out his instructions. His first clash with the Rebels came August 29–30, 1862, in the Second Battle of Bull Run. He and fellow Union soldiers encountered Southern generals Robert E. Lee and Thomas Jonathan "Stonewall" Jackson. During the battle, Ranald suffered wounds in both shoulders.

Twenty hours after dropping from his wounds, Mackenzie welcomed the medical detachment that picked him up where he had fallen and carried him to an emergency hospital in Washington. Catherine Mackenzie visited her son the next day.

"I am wounded in the back, but I wasn't running away," he hastened to explain.

The unofficial promotion to first lieutenant, which Mackenzie received for "gallant and meritorious service" during the battle, proved to his family that his slight frame had not prevented success on his first test as a soldier. The events connected with his first battle also represented a forecast of what would come in the young man's three years of Civil War service.

After recovering from his wounds, he saw action in nearly every major battle of the war, from the autumn of 1862 up to and including Lee's surrender to Grant at Appomattox Courthouse on April 12, 1865. These included Fredericksburg, Chancellorsville, Gettysburg, the Wilderness, Spotsylvania, Cold Harbor, and Petersburg. He also helped defend Washington, D.C., and later participated in the Shenandoah Valley campaign with Gen. Philip Sheridan, fighting battles at Winchester, Cedar Creek, Opequon, Fisher's Hill, and Middleton, Virginia. The battles of White Oak Road and Five Forks in the Richmond campaign became Mackenzie's final clashes with Confederates, for the war neared its close.

The three years of fighting begun at Bull Run took a heavy toll on Mackenzie's slender frame. He sustained six wounds, including the loss of the two middle fingers on his right hand.

His honorary promotion for gallantry, in August of 1862, was the first of seven awarded him during the three years of his participation in the war. A month before the surrender, his superiors officially promoted Mackenzie to brigadier general in the regular army. Four days later, he received the honorary rank of brevet major general of volunteers. The twenty-four-year-old major general took time off to have a picture made for his family. He was at that time a young man of 145 pounds and

11

medium height. Long sideburns framed the strong and sensitive features of his handsome but serious face. He possessed a determined chin and mirthless eyes and mouth. Being a soldier was serious business with him, and he wanted the men who served under him to feel the same way. Consequently, he was a rigid disciplinarian.

At one time during the fighting, as a mutiny brewed among his men, the young brevet major general came very close to repeating the history made by his father. For two years, Mackenzie had performed engineering duties, always having bridges and crossings ready in advance of the arrival of the Union soldiers. The routine duty tired him, and he became anxious to command a fighting unit. Finally the opportunity came as he replaced the commander of a Connecticut volunteer unit who had been killed. The men of the unit had enlisted together with their officers in Connecticut, and had remained close friends. Young Mackenzie, their new commander, was an outsider who remained aloof and who quickly instituted strict discipline. Because of his strict punishments and his irritability. Mackenzie's men became more afraid of him than of the Rebel grapeshot and canister. The lives of hundreds of men depended on his judgment and ability. Constant awareness of this fact made the sensitive young leader extremely tense when facing danger for himself and his men.

Before the Shenandoah Valley campaign, Mackenzie's men circulated a rumor in the regiment that their commander would be "disposed of" in the next battle because they disliked him so thoroughly. A stray bullet from his own ranks was supposed to kill Mackenzie "accidentally." At the Battle of Winchester, the plot fell through because of the young commander's outstanding courage. He galloped up and down at the head of his men, with his hat on his saber, through a hailstorm of lead. The men held their fire, assuming Mackenzie would be hit soon by the enemy anyway. After several minutes had passed and he still remained alive, none of his men dared take a shot at so brave a man. Finally, an enemy shell cut his horse apart, and Mackenzie suffered serious wounds. But he refused to leave the field, even at the request of his commanding general, Philip Sheridan.

Following the battle, the opinion of his men concerning him became completely reversed. They swore by their brave young leader through the final months of the war.

As opposing sides lined up in the open field before Appomattox Courthouse for Grant to accept Lee's surrender, the Union commander ordered Mackenzie to take charge of surrendered Confederate property. The war had ended for the young major general who rose to higher rank during the war than any other man in his graduating class at West Point.

Mackenzie's family would finally have to admit his success as a soldier. But now that the fighting was over, what could such a man do after reaching what seemed to be the pinnacle of his career in only three years?

For the time being, he stayed in the Army. Grant could not afford to send all of his Union soldiers home because he needed their presence to maintain the peace so recently won. Mackenzie commanded the cavalry in the Department of Virginia for the next three and one-half months. Following that duty, he returned to his family in New York City to await orders. He was mustered out of the service in January 1866 as a brigadier general of volunteers.

Chapter Four

The Call of the West

During his extended leave with his family in New York, the twenty-five-year-old "retired" brigadier general had plenty of time to read the eastern newspapers. A highlight of the big-city weeklies was the report, usually on page one, dealing with another war — a continuing war that raged on the western frontier between citizens of the United States and "wild Indians."

To a man whose very existence for three years had been saturated with the actions of two sides challenging each other to the death, day after day, life with relatives in New York became boring. It certainly lacked the exciting diversion offered by the West. There, Indians who had been pushed westward until they had no other place to go were skirmishing with the hordes of white men who were invading their domain. Ever-multiplying throngs of white settlers moved to the land whose gates had been opened to them by the Homestead Act of 1862. That act promised 160 acres of free land to each head of a household if he would live on it and improve it for five years.

Still other gates were opening as Ranald Mackenzie read his *New York Times* in 1866. Workers of the Union

Pacific and Central Pacific railroads pushed to complete iron rails to connect the continent. The prospect of such modern transportation drew many settlers and workers westward, further angering the Native Americans. Following the close of the war, Southern families whose homes and farms had been destroyed by the fighting packed up their few remaining belongings and moved westward to a new land and a new hope. Even many Northerners, tired of plowing and planting worn-out land that bore few crops, and weary of working in soot-filled factories, struck out for the West to claim the earliest Americans' land as their own. What began as a few skirmishes between Native Americans and settlers over territory that would extend the United States from ocean to ocean would erupt eventually into full-scale war.

To a man whose proven attributes included raw courage and accurate military judgment, the prospect of engaging in the western war must have been inviting. Mackenzie ignored the fact that his physical qualifications for continued fighting did not seem to measure up.

The peacetime Army possessed too many generals, created during the Civil War by frequent field promotions such as Mackenzie's. If he decided to remain in the service, Mackenzie would have to go back to a lower rank. But the U.S. Army represented his chosen career — his life — and he rejoined. After all, the Army did need soldiers to protect the western settlers.

Young Mackenzie returned to duty in February 1866 as a captain of engineers. He performed construction work at Portsmouth Harbor, New Hampshire. This was the same type of engineering duty he had grown tired of during the first two years of his service in the war. He soon requested transfer to the West. Months passed, however, with Capt. Ranald Mackenzie still engaged in construction work in New Hampshire.

In March 1867, the chance to transfer to the West finally came. The position of colonel of the Forty-first Infantry (stationed in Baton Rouge, Louisiana, but soon to move to Texas) became available. Several other officers turned down the assignment when they learned that the Forty-first consisted of inexperienced African-American troopers who a few years previously had been Southern slaves.

The thought of a young man like Mackenzie, weakened by six wounds, turning muscular field hands into soldiers probably seemed impossible to many people. His family no doubt felt the same as they had when he decided ten years earlier to substitute a military career for one in law. Mackenzie attacked the challenge, determined to prove his abilities again to those who doubted.

Once in Texas, with the competent help of his mild-mannered lieutenant colonel, the stocky, walrus-mustached William R. Shafter, Ranald built the Forty-first Infantry into one of the best black regiments in the Army. The Indians called the African-American soldiers "buffalo soldiers," because their kinky hair reminded the Indians of the huge, shaggy beasts they hunted. These "buffalo soldiers," accustomed to taking orders from former masters on Southern plantations, adjusted readily to taking orders from their United States Army commander, Colonel Mackenzie. He drilled them, taught them fighting skills, and insisted upon strict discipline.

Problems emerged when the black soldiers descended upon white frontier towns, but Mackenzie dealt justly with these incidents. He felt Indian raids to be the real problem. Desperately, Mackenzie wanted permission to take his men out on scouting forays against the Lipan Apaches, Kickapoos, and half-breed Mexicans who raided the southern border of Texas. But the orders that came to him instructed him to build or repair various Federal forts located along the southern and western frontier.

During the Civil War, while most of the men fought the North, Indians had raided and burned homesteads and forts in western Texas as they resisted white encroachment. They had pushed back the settled area forty or fifty miles along the thousand-mile frontier line stretching from north to south through Texas. Settlers had packed up and moved to communities in eastern Texas during the war, when little or no protection existed. Now that the war had ended, Federal troops returned to Texas, as represented by Mackenzie's Forty-first Infantry and several companies of the Sixth and Tenth cavalries.

Army officials in Washington believed that Mackenzie's troopers, as former slaves, would be more suited to constructing or repairing forts along this frontier line than to fighting Indians. Besides, there existed all that engineering experience of their commander.

After two years of such construction tasks, Mackenzie and his troopers pulled garrison duty at Fort McKavett in south central Texas. Previously they had built corrals for the cavalry horses, repaired the barracks for the men, and renovated the kitchen, guard house, and outbuildings. They also enlarged and practically rebuilt the officers' quarters at McKavett.

Finally, Mackenzie commanded two companies of the Ninth Cavalry along with his three companies of the Forty-first Infantry. With the cavalry he could at last do a little scouting for Indians.

During Mackenzie's years spent near the southern border of Texas, a change in the Indian policy of the United States occurred in Washington. Upon taking office as president in 1869, former Union commander Ulysses S. Grant instituted a new policy toward the Native Americans which he believed would solve all problems and begin a new era of brotherhood between the red and white races. He placed members of religious denominations over Indian agencies throughout the West. Grant reasoned that they should be able to deal more kindly with the Native Americans and not mistreat them. Another reason he wanted religious men appointed was to break up the "Indian Ring" whereby agents receiving a salary of $1,800 a year could retire with immense fortunes after a few years because of their improper use of Indian funds. Grant assumed that the religious men could be trusted not to enrich themselves by giving shoddy goods to the Indians. Because members of the Quaker religion volunteered as agents, the policy thus begun by President Grant became popularly known as his "Quaker Peace Policy." These Indian agents served under the authority of the secretary of the interior rather than the War Department.

The policy appeared to be a humane way of dealing with the Indian tribes. But the important question was, would it work? Would it keep the Native Americans on their reservations and stop the raiding? Most easterners, far removed from the actual situation, praised the success of Grant's program. But western frontiersmen, seeing their homes and loved ones destroyed by red men who were fed and supplied arms by the government on the reservations, pronounced the policy an absolute failure.

Col. Ranald Mackenzie, stationed at Fort McKavett in south central Texas, saw firsthand that the Quaker Peace Policy did not work. He suggested that the power of the military should be used to restrain the Indians on their reservations.

In his own assigned area of Texas he did what he could to protect the settlers. But until the government employed the force of the military along the entire frontier, permanent peace would remain impossible.

Part II

In Texas: 1869–1873

Chapter Five

Colonel of the Fourth Cavalry

Military details and red tape, which prevented a soldier from doing the job he was supposed to be doing, irritated Ranald Mackenzie. On his desk lay an order for court-martial duty at the headquarters of the Department of Texas in San Antonio. Periodically, officers were assigned the task of serving on a military board to discipline soldiers who engaged in drunken brawls, deserted, or committed similar misdemeanors. Only occasionally was the crime of sufficient importance to be really worth taking an officer from his command post, Mackenzie believed. The order meant that Colonel Mackenzie would be away from his post at Fort McKavett several weeks.

His days while in San Antonio were consumed by the monotonous court-martial proceedings as he heard case after case that the military saved until the periodic convening of the board of officers. Evenings at the Tunstall boardinghouse on Elm Street did not prove quite so boring. F. P. Tunstall, owner of the establishment, was the father of a beautiful eighteen-year-old daughter named Florida. Though ordinarily shy around women, Macken-

20

zie gradually lost much of his timidity around the lively, friendly girl. He began to enjoy his stay in San Antonio, which stretched on for several weeks. The old Spanish city seemed to contribute an atmosphere of romance as he passed through the streets on his way to post headquarters northwest of town. Once there and in his place, Mackenzie felt that the droning monotony of Army justice seemed unending. He wanted the daily proceedings to conclude quickly so that he could spend more time with Florida.

When the time came to return to Fort McKavett, Mackenzie discovered that he could find sufficient time and excuse to make the 200-mile round trip from his command post to San Antonio to visit the lovely Florida. He made several such trips, until the day arrived several months later when Florida informed him that she had become engaged to an Army doctor, Dr. Redford Sharpe, who was stationed in San Antonio. Mackenzie knew the man. Sharpe was nineteen years older than Florida and eight years older than Ranald.

Florida's approaching marriage shattered the young colonel's self-esteem. He mourned that he had nothing better to offer her than the uncomfortable life on a far western Army post. Married to Dr. Sharpe, she would not have to leave her comfortable San Antonio. Mackenzie rode westward to his command post with his heart still in the Alamo City.

Back at Fort McKavett, he devoted his time to protecting the area surrounding his command from marauding Indians. He sent two expeditions of his Ninth Cavalry to the upper reaches of the Brazos River.

As commander of the subdistrict of the Pecos, Mackenzie made a formal inspection of Fort Concho, located northwest of McKavett. There he saw his former lieutenant colonel, walrus-mustached Bill Shafter. Mackenzie sent out an expedition of a hundred men from Concho to the northwest to hunt Indians. When they returned a month later, after a two-day battle with their prey, he ordered out a larger force of 150. They also engaged the Indians in October 1869, captured their horses, burned their camp, and killed nearly a hundred braves.

The colonel was disappointed that he could not lead the expeditions personally. However, routine inspection tours and census-taking of frontier counties occupied his time and military chores. He used his authority to keep scouting parties active in the field, so conditions in the area began to improve.

Florida Tunstall Sharpe, nestled safely in her home in San Antonio, no doubt had occasion to read the article in the November 26, 1869, issue of the *San Antonio Daily Herald* which stated that "had Texas a few more Mackenzies to guard her frontier there would be no occasion for atrocities by Indians."

An opportunity for Ranald to see more action in the field came in the fall of 1870, when he traveled to Washington to appear on a special military board. While there he received a new appointment, on December 14, 1870, to command the Fourth Cavalry, a unit that was scattered among at least nine different posts along the southern and western frontier.

After a two-month leave with his family in New York, Mackenzie assumed command of his new unit at Fort Concho in February 1871. For many of the old career soldiers of the Fourth it was a new experience to serve under a slim, clean-shaven young commander, especially when he revealed from the beginning that he intended to be a stern and exacting taskmaster.

Soon after accepting command of Fort Concho, the colonel received orders to move his men to Fort Richardson, the northernmost post on the Texas frontier, near Jacksboro. Shortly after Mackenzie and the headquarters unit of the Fourth Cavalry arrived at Fort Richardson, an example of the colonel's strictness and of resulting improved conditions occurred. Jacksboro in mid-April of 1871 was a tough cattle town made rougher by the fact that an Army post lay a half mile away. Soldiers of the

Sixth Cavalry were ready to move north to Kansas, and their replacements of the Fourth already had arrived. Ten companies of men after the April payday gambled, drank, and brawled in Jacksboro's saloons. The Old Wichita Saloon alone took in $10,000 after that payday. Fortunately, the Sixth soon moved out to Kansas.

Cowboys liked to ride down Jacksboro's only street each night and fire six-shooters at windows. The colonel soon put a stop to roughhouse activity by letting offenders cool off overnight in the post guardhouse. The fact that he was arresting civilians did not stop Mackenzie if the offenders disrupted the peace near his fort. Peace-loving civilians naturally appreciated the newfound quiet and praised their young post commander.

Fort Richardson's previous commander, Col. James Oakes of the Sixth Cavalry, reportedly drove around the post in his carriage with his face masked to preserve his complexion. Mackenzie, however, soon became known for leading his men out on scouting forays in search of Indians to protect the local citizens from frequent raids. It was no wonder that his fame began to spread throughout Texas as the bold young leader of the Fourth Cavalry.

Chapter Six

General Sherman's Visit

C ol. Ranald Mackenzie sat at his desk at Fort Richardson waiting for his adjutant to report to him. The sun of a bright mid-May day streamed through the open window of his office in the picket structure. The adjutant, 2nd Lt. Robert Carter, a young West Point graduate, had arrived on the frontier with his bride only a month earlier. When Carter reported, Mackenzie ordered him to choose fifteen men from the regiment and proceed on the road to Fort Griffin to meet Gen. William T. Sherman. The general, who headed the entire United States Army in Washington, was making an inspection tour of the Texas frontier posts.

When General Sherman rode through the gate of Fort Richardson at about sunset the following day, practically everyone in Jacksboro, the town on the opposite side of Lost Creek, lined up to greet him. Several citizens waited in Mackenzie's office to protest to the general about frequent Indian raids and to request additional military protection for their frontier. General Sherman had received many letters from Texans making such requests. He assumed that the people only wanted more soldiers because local citizens made money from government contracts to feed the men and their animals. He purposely made the frontier tour of May 1871 to determine the true situation for himself.

The citizens told him that a farmer couldn't even go into town for supplies and know that his house and family would be safe until he returned. Another said that not a family in those parts had escaped some tragedy dealt by the Indians.

Several deaths had occurred in April near Fort Richardson. Typical of such raids was one in which four members of the Cambron family had been killed and their bodies mutilated in Jack County on Lost Creek. A neighbor, John Lynn, discovered the bodies and found two tiny children alive when he came on a visit. Arriving home with the children, Lynn found all of his own family dead, killed by a band of Indians skirting the fringes of the frontier. In the same raid the Indians killed members of two other families, the Jones and Babb families, and took three prisoners from the Babb home.

General Sherman listened politely to the complaints of the citizens of Jacksboro, but shook his head incredulously. He promised them, however, that he would look into the matter when he arrived at Fort Sill on the Comanche-Kiowa reservation in Indian Territory. He said he would investigate their charges that the Indians had obtained arms and ammunition at the post and then used them on their raids in Texas.

General Sherman declined Mackenzie's offer to share the colonel's quarters and ordered his escort of men to pitch his tent as he had been doing throughout his trip.

Fort Richardson and its inhabitants settled down for the night. Toward morning a wounded man limped in, shot in the right foot. Soldiers took him to the post hospital, where he received attention and began telling a frightening story of a raid by more than a hundred Kiowas at Salt Creek Prairie the previous afternoon. Salt Creek Prairie was located some twenty-two miles west of Fort Richardson.

The man, named Thomas Brazeal, explained that he worked as a teamster on a ten-wagon train driving corn from Weatherford to Fort Griffin. Of the twelve teamsters, he knew that seven lay dead at the wagons. The other men ran into the brush as he did.

Early the next morning General Sherman visited the hospital and heard Brazeal's story. The general became somewhat excited when he learned the time of the attack. He and his small escort of seventeen men had passed Salt Creek Prairie themselves only a short time earlier. Sherman remembered that one of his men had reported seeing an Indian, but the others in the escort laughed at the man for imagining he saw an Indian so near the fort.

The perpetrators had lain in wait several hours for the wagon train of corn and for the forty mules pulling it. They had not attacked the military detachment because they saw no point in antagonizing the government, which provided their food and supplies on the reservation. Sherman began to get a clearer understanding of the Kiowas than he could from his desk in Washington.

The general wasted no time worrying over the close scrape he and his men had experienced. To a career Army man, danger meant an increased sense of duty. While it heightened his senses, it also made him even more determined to do his job. Sherman knew that Fort Richardson's commander, Colonel Mackenzie, was such a man. Sherman sent a courier to Fort Griffin with a message for Col. W. H. Wood at that post to meet Colonel Mackenzie at the scene of the attack within two days with 100 cavalrymen. He told Mackenzie to take 150 troopers of his Fourth Cavalry, with twenty days' rations, and leave immediately.

Sherman's orders were: "If the Indians have crossed the Red River, enter the Comanche-Kiowa Reservation. And if the trail be fresh and you should overtake the party anywhere within thirty or forty miles of the Red River, you will not hesitate to attack the party, secure the property stolen, and any other property or stock in their possession, and bring them to me at Fort Sill."

Mackenzie sent an advance detachment and planned to follow quickly with four companies of his Fourth Cavalry equipped for many days in the field. Meanwhile, citizens of Jacksboro paid $50 to a twenty-two-year-old young man named Henry Strong to go to Weatherford to get Henry Warren, the owner of the wagon train that had been attacked. Young Strong possessed more courage than his small, skinny body suggested, to venture out alone almost as quickly as the advance guard of the Army. Strong rode 112 miles on two horses in twelve hours. When he returned to Fort Richardson, Mackenzie was ready to start after the Indians with four companies of cavalry, so Strong decided to go along. A Jacksboro citizen named Jim Dozier served as official Army guide on the expedition. Henry Warren also wanted to accompany Mackenzie to try to recover his mules.

The dark clouds that had threatened all day finally combined, and the storm broke. Rain poured down, thunder roared, and the post became illuminated as bright as afternoon during the brief flashes of lightning. The blue-uniformed troopers of Companies A, B, C, and F of the Fourth Cavalry lined up on the parade ground, ready to begin the scouting expedition. Several pack animals reared on their haunches as the thunder clapped, and their burdens fell off and had to be replaced. The troopers realized that several days' field duty stood between them and their soft, dry beds at the fort.

By the time Mackenzie and his four companies of cavalrymen from Fort Richardson reached the scene of the attack, a deluge of water had obliterated the Indians' trail. Bodies of seven teamsters, swollen and bloated, lay in several inches of water. One charred body of a teamster lay chained to a wagon wheel, and all wagons had been burned. Whether or not the man had been dead when the wagon burned, Mackenzie could not determine.

27

The colonel wrote a report to General Sherman, who planned to proceed on to Fort Sill: "I reached here about dark and find statements concerning the wagon train not exaggerated. Five mules lay dead around the wagons. The sergeant in charge of the detail, who was sent out in advance, found seven men about the wagons with heads split open and badly mutilated otherwise. Captain Wilson stated that the scalps of all had been taken with the exception of one bald-headed victim."

While Colonel Mackenzie waited for the command of Fort Griffin to join him, he ordered his men to dig a huge grave. The soldiers began digging, but had to dip water out of it repeatedly because of the continuous rain. When they finished digging, the soldiers placed all seven bodies together in a charred wagon bed and shoveled dirt over them. They covered the grave with rocks to keep buzzards and animals away. Mackenzie suggested that the men cut seven marks on one of the larger stones to show the number of persons buried there.

Then for two tiresome weeks, Mackenzie and his men searched for the guilty Indians who had participated in the raid. The rain had turned western Texas into a sloppy, sticky bog, making the muddy trail impossible to follow. Mackenzie led his men all the way up to Fort Sill in Indian Territory without finding any Indians.

General Sherman had remained at Fort Richardson and on May 19 had greeted another delegation of citizens who begged for his help. The crowd of several hundred frontier people from around Jacksboro were there to protest the Indian attack. Some asked if they could accompany the general to Fort Sill to recover property stolen from them by the Indians. Sherman told them they could.

Sherman and his entourage arrived at Fort Sill on May 23, after traveling the 123 miles from Fort Richardson. Fort Sill was located near the Comanche-Kiowa reservation in Indian Territory. The Wichita Mountains extended from the northwest corner of the reservation westward for fifty miles.

Lawrie Tatum, a slick-headed Quaker whom the Indians called Bald Head, served as Indian agent on the reservation. When Tatum called on Sherman soon after the general's arrival at Fort Sill, Sherman briefed him on the Salt Creek Massacre and asked if any of his charges had left the reservations. Tatum replied that he did not know but would check. The agent admitted that he realized the necessity of a more vigorous policy of punishment toward the rebellious Kiowas and Comanches.

Four days later, several Kiowa chiefs appeared at Tatum's office to request their usual rations. While there they bragged of a raid into Texas. The most outspoken, named Satanta, claimed the honor of leading the raid. Tatum told his charges that a "Great White Father" from Washington visited at Fort Sill and wanted to see them. Then the agent sent a message to Sherman asking him to arrest the guilty chiefs when they arrived for their conference.

Sherman met the chiefs on the verandah of the officers' quarters. Behind him, hidden by closed shutters, stood African-American troopers of the Tenth Cavalry with carbines loaded. They were ready to protect Sherman in case the Kiowas caused trouble.

Sherman told Satanta, who spoke for the group, that they would be arrested and taken to Texas for a murder trial. The large Kiowa's bragging stopped, and he put his hands in the air and hollered, "Don't shoot," as he saw Sherman meant it. Several of the group ran for the gate, including Lone Wolf and Eagle Heart. The Tenth cavalrymen restrained three Kiowas — Satanta, Satank, and Big Tree.

Satanta, in his late fifties, was in excellent physical condition and held a reputation for oratory in his tribe. Satank, a short, lean Indian in his late sixties, had high cheekbones, prominent nose and chin, a scraggly mustache, and a harsh glare. He had pulled out all his eyelashes and painted the edges of his eyelids with vermillion. The third Kiowa, Big Tree, was a very short, full-cheeked nineteen- or twenty-year-old subchief of Satank's.

Troopers of the Tenth Cavalry stationed at Fort Sill placed the three Kiowas in a cellar under the officers' quarters for safekeeping until Colonel Mackenzie arrived with his men to transfer the prisoners to Jacksboro for a civilian trial. Although this would be an unusual procedure, perhaps a first, these were General Sherman's instructions. The Indians waited in confinement nine days. Sherman proceeded northward to complete his tour of the frontier, reach the railroad in Kansas, and travel back to Washington.

Tired and disappointed from his unsuccessful attempt to locate the guilty Indians, Mackenzie led his men into Fort Sill after two weeks in the field. He became somewhat cheered when he learned that Sherman had apprehended the Kiowa chiefs.

After allowing his men and himself four days to rest, Mackenzie prepared to leave Indian Territory for Texas. He ordered the transfer of the three Kiowas from their basement guardhouse to wagons for transport to Texas. At the start of the trip, Satank struggled with the soldiers and tried to escape. When he saw the wagons, he refused to budge, mouthing his hatred for his white captors. The young Kiowa, Big Tree, managed to calm his chief into a restrained march to the wagons. Had Big Tree not intervened, the old Kiowa might have forced the soldiers to shoot him on the spot. As a result of Satank's contrariness, soldiers threw him into a wagon by himself, while they allowed Big Tree and Satanta to ride together in a second wagon.

Colonel Mackenzie sent his men ahead with the three chiefs heavily guarded in the two wagons, while he remained behind to confer briefly with the commander of Fort Sill, Col. B. H. Grierson.

Chapter Seven

Trial of the Kiowas

O ld Satank served as head man in the warrior society of the Kiowa tribe, the Kaitsenko. The order consisted of only ten members, brave men chosen and pledged to lead every desperate charge and to keep their place in the front of every battle until they won victory or death.

In battle their leader carried a specially made arrow and wore over his left shoulder a black elkskin sash, the end of which trailed on the ground. When his men prepared to charge the enemy, a Kaitsenko warrior thrust the arrow through the tail of the sash, pinning the leader to the ground. Thus he must remain, defying the enemy, until the Kiowa warriors had driven them from the field or, if the warriors were retreating, until his comrades set him free by pulling the arrow from the ground. If no one remembered to release him, honor dictated that the leader remain and fight to the death. If he pulled up the arrow himself, he became the laughingstock of the tribe. Therefore, on the trip to Texas, Chief Satank, the leading warrior of his tribe, apparently felt that his obligations required him to defy the whites.

31

When he knew definitely that he was traveling to Texas for trial, Satank began a loud harangue to the two guards in the wagon with him, telling them that a great chief and warrior should not be treated so roughly. Pointing toward a lone tree beside the road about a mile from the post, Satank predicted that he would never go beyond it. He then told a passing Caddo Indian, "Tell my people I died the first day out. Tell them to gather my bones from the side of the road and bury them."

Raising his voice and pulling a blanket over his head, he sang his death song: *"Iha hyo oya iya iya o iha yaya yoyo. Aheya aheya yaheyo ya eye heyo eheyo."* ("Oh, Sun, you remain forever, but we Kaitsenko must die. Oh, Earth, you remain forever, but we Kaitsenko must die.")

At about the time that his wagon came even with the lone tree, the rebellious old chief threw back the blanket, pulled a concealed knife from his breechcloth, and stabbed a soldier in the wagon with him. He grabbed the soldier's gun, fired a shot and tried to fire another, but the gun jammed.

Cpl. John B. Charlton, a young giant of a man, shot Satank twice, and the Indian fell off the wagon by the side of the road, near the tree to which he had pointed.

Mackenzie rode up about this time from Fort Sill, wanting to know what caused the moving column of soldiers and wagons to stop only a mile from the fort. After hearing the story, Mackenzie told his soldiers to lay Satank under the lone tree by the side of the road, even as the old Kiowa had predicted. Reservation Indians who heard the commotion already were arriving to mourn over his body and prepare it for burial.

Mackenzie instructed his men to guard the other two Kiowas closely during the remainder of the trip so another incident could not occur. At night he placed pickets and outposts far out to prevent surprise attacks. He feared that the Kiowas, upon learning that soldiers took their chiefs to Texas to be tried for murder, might attempt their rescue. Each night, soldiers secured the two

Kiowas by stretching them on their backs and fastening their legs and arms widely apart to stakes driven in the ground. Mackenzie assigned men to fan the numerous mosquitoes away. Swarms of the bothersome insects hovered in the creek bottoms where the command naturally camped each night to be near water for their animals.

Mackenzie and his weary Fourth Cavalry troopers arrived at Fort Richardson on a clear day in mid-June. A huge crowd came out to see them and the Indians. Satanta became the center of attention. He appeared to be more than six feet tall because of the small pony upon which he rode. The two prisoners no longer rode in the wagons. Naked except for a breechcloth and beaded moccasins, Satanta carried a scalp lock adorned by an eagle feather. His muscles stood out as he sat proud and erect, looking like a bronze statue. The fact that his feet were lashed under the horse's belly and dust covered his jet black hair did not detract from his regal appearance. Big Tree appeared less important than Satanta by comparison, which he actually was, being a much younger subchief, or orderly.

Mackenzie turned over the prisoners to Sheriff Michael McMillan for protection from the angry citizens of Jacksboro until the trial, which began three weeks later. The case became the first known trial of Native Americans in a white man's court. Cowboys, farmers, and merchants from Jacksboro comprised the twelve jurors who lined up on wooden benches to hear the case.

The wounded teamster, Thomas Brazeal, served as a witness for the state, as did Indian Agent Lawrie Tatum from Fort Sill, and Colonel Mackenzie. The colonel told what he and his men had found upon arriving at the Salt Creek site in May.

Prosecuting Attorney Samuel W. T. Lanham, who later became a governor of Texas, spoke long and forcefully: "Had it not been for General Sherman and his most opportune journey through this section, and his personal observation of this dire tragedy, it may well be doubted whether these brutes in human shape would ever have been brought to trial. We are greatly indebted to the military arm of the government for kindly offices and cooperation in procuring the arrest and transference of the defendants. If the entire management of the Indian question were submitted to that gallant and distinguished Army officer General Mackenzie who graces this occasion with his dignified presence, our frontier would soon enjoy immunity from these marauders."

Later, Judge Charles Soward gave Satanta permission to speak. The chief made a speech in Kiowa, broken Spanish, and English, which the Fort Sill interpreter translated for spectators: "I am suffering now for the crimes of bad Indians — of Satank and Lone Wolf and Kicking Bird and Big Bow and Fast Bear and Eagle Heart, and if you will let me go, I will kill the three latter with my own hand. I did not kill the Texans. I came down Pease River as a big medicine man to doctor the wounds of the braves. I am a big chief among my people, and have great influence among the warriors of my tribe — they know my voice and will hear my word. If you will let me go back to my people I will withdraw my warriors from Texas. I will take them all across Red River and that will be the line between us and the pale faces. I will wash out the spots of blood and make it a white land, and there shall be peace, and the Texans may plow and drive their oxen to the river, but if you kill me it will be a spark on the prairie — make big fire — burn heap."

Two defense attorneys were assigned to the chiefs and sincerely defended their Indian charges. The main argument was that the Native Americans were defending their land from white encroachment.

Judge Soward took a long time to charge the jury. He told them to deliberate the things they had heard in the court and to render a verdict. When the twelve jurymen retired to consider the case, they simply formed a huddle in a corner of the room cleared for them. They conferred only a short while before filing back to their chairs with a verdict of guilty. A riot probably would have ensued had the Indians been freed. Judge Soward sentenced them to be executed by hanging on the first day of September.

Immediately after the trial, Agent Tatum from the Kiowa reservation asked the judge to commute the sentence to imprisonment rather than death. If the chiefs were simply imprisoned, he explained, the reservation Indians might behave in hopes of securing their release. If the two Kiowas were hanged, however, the Indians might instigate new hostilities in retaliation.

The judge said that he no longer controlled the fate of the two Kiowas. The governor of Texas was the only one who now could commute the sentence. Tatum wrote the Texas governor, Edmund J. Davis. Other officials requested the same thing, so Governor Davis complied. Texas citizens on the frontier protested furiously, demanding that the Indians should be hanged.

Colonel Mackenzie did some writing of his own that summer. Even before the trial he wrote Gen. J. J. Reynolds, who was commander of the Department of Texas, and General Sherman, informing them of the need for an expedition against the Indians, who, like Satanta and Big Tree, kept leaving the reservation to raid. He told Sherman: "The Kiowas and Comanches are entirely beyond any control and have been for a long time. Mr. Tatum . . . is anxious that the Kiowas and Comanches now out of control be brought under. This can be accomplished only by the Army . . . Either these Indians must be punished or they must be allowed to murder and rob at their own discretion."

In July, orders arrived telling Mackenzie to proceed into the field as soon as possible. Reading his new orders, Mackenzie hoped for more success than he had known on his last expedition in the field. At that time someone else had apprehended the guilty Indians that his own expedition should have captured.

Chapter Eight

A Scorching Expedition

"I t's on fire! The prairie's on fire!"
Mackenzie heard the frantic shouts from the enlisted men's camp and became alert instantly. Whitish smoke circled upward from the six-foot-high orange flames beyond the camp. Men bolted to their feet, rolled up bedding, and ran for their frightened horses. The screams of the rearing, stomping animals combined with the yelling of the men had created a scene of loud confusion.

The fire came from canebrakes, which stretched for several miles south of their campsite. The brakes crackled and sent up a scorching blaze. Wind blew the growing flames toward camp. Not since the downpouring of late May, which had ruined their field expedition after the Salt Creek attack, had any moisture blessed the area. The dried and sunburnt grass blazed rapidly under the August sun.

Mackenzie directed his men to move to the dry bed of the Red River to protect themselves from the onrush of the flames. If Indians had set the fire, which seemed likely, they might try to attack when the command seemed most confused.

The men cursed the flames and the Indians whom they deemed responsible. The infantry in charge of the supply wagons struggled with their creaking, cracking vehicles. Their whips kept the tired mules moving up the dry, rocky creek bed. The wagons swayed and groaned fourteen miles more before Mackenzie, as weary as any of his men, ordered a halt and prepared to camp a second time for the night. Their site this time was West Cache Creek. No attack came from the Indians.

The next day the colonel led his expedition twelve miles farther west of the Red River, where he met Col. B. H. Grierson, commander at Fort Sill. Grierson also was leading an expedition in search of Indians absent from the reservation. The two commanders conferred.

Colonel Grierson agreed to cover the territory nearest Fort Sill and to move around in the country between the Wichita Mountains and the North Fork of the Red River. This left Mackenzie with the southern and western part of the Texas Panhandle area. He planned to operate in the badlands between the North Fork and the Salt Fork of the Red River.

The two expeditions camped together that night as their two commanders enjoyed a meal and continued their conference. The next day, however, the two columns of blue-coated troopers moved out in different directions. Mackenzie moved his men twelve and fifteen miles each day. When his Tonkawa scouts reported Indian signs, the colonel hurried his men in the direction shown by the scouts, sometimes marching all night to try to overtake the renegade Kiowas.

One night the cavalry horses stampeded. The men in the command, including their colonel, thought the Indians had caused it. Only the surgeon of the expedition knew that the Indians had not. Earlier, he had been unable to sleep and had stepped out of his tent in his night shirt. The surgeon's moving white figure had frightened a nearby horse, and it reared up and whinnied. This action scared the other horses and triggered the stampede. Not until thirty years later did the doctor reveal what he had caused — so afraid was he of Mackenzie.

A dispatch rider approached Mackenzie's command one day with messages for the colonel, who read the notes quickly. Reynolds had approved his request for a fall expedition in the field. But then Mackenzie came upon a disturbing dispatch. He read a copy of a letter from General Sherman sent to General Reynolds at Texas headquarters in San Antonio. Sherman said that Mackenzie "should abide by Reynolds' order of July 5 not to cross the boundary of Texas into the Indian country unless called upon by Grierson, as the latter possessed ample force to deal with the Kiowas." A notation on the letter from General Reynolds told Mackenzie he had "no authority to enter the reservations unless in actual pursuit."

Mackenzie became upset by the letter and wondered how the federal government expected him to punish the Indians who had left the reservation to raid in Texas if, meanwhile, it restricted his activities. It seemed useless to lead his men back and forth in an area where no Indians existed, while he was denied the right to enter Grierson's territory, which clearly held more sign of Native Americans.

For several hours after receiving the dispatch, Mackenzie remained thoughtful and uncommunicative with his men. He wanted to do a good job of protecting the frontier in his area of command. To do this he must decisively defeat the Indians who were leaving the reservation to raid and kill near Fort Richardson. How could he do this if General Sherman restricted his activities? Mackenzie was not allowed to follow a fresh Indian trail if he found one, if it led into Grierson's area of command. Grierson was not the type of commander to instigate action against the Indians. Mackenzie knew this and so did Sherman. Washington leaders clearly did not want any hostile action against the Indians at this time for fear that such action would hamper its attempt to maintain the Quaker Peace Policy toward the Indians. Apparently, the Indian commissioners in Washington had influenced Sherman since his return. It seemed silly to Mackenzie to spend all the money and effort on a field expedition after hostile Indians, with no intention of punishing them for being off the reservation. He knew one thing: His orders said to punish any Indians found raiding in Texas. The citizens of that state expected him to do so, and he intended to attack — if he could find any Indians.

For two more weeks Mackenzie operated in the area south of the North Fork, between it and the Elm Fork of the Red River. The rough and sun-parched country possessed half-dried streams contaminated by buffalo excrement and gypsum. Gypsum, a whitish mineral found plentifully in the area, crusted on the men's clothes and on their canteens. Mackenzie and many of the men became ill from drinking the putrid water. Cramps, vomiting, and diarrhea weakened them. The briny water caused the men to be even more thirsty than they were before they drank it. Alkali in the water caused cutting and bleeding of the men's lips.

Mackenzie suffered as much as any of his men, but he tried to be cheerful about it for the sake of morale.

"Gentlemen," he said, "we shall all have a new stomach when it gets thoroughly coated with a crust of gypsum." Measuring on his finger, he added, "I think my coating is now about that thick." As soon as he took a swallow of the black concoction that represented coffee, he jumped up and ran to the bushes to dispose of it. When he came back, someone slyly asked him, "What is the matter?"

"Oh, heap sick! Heap sick!" he said with a weak smile that was intended as a laugh.

Riding in the blazing August sun each day became almost unbearable. The men strained their eyes in the glare, and gun barrels became so hot that everyone's hands blistered from touching the weapons. Mackenzie ordered each man to place a damp sponge in his hat to prevent heatstroke, and to carry an extra canteen so that the sponge could be moistened at intervals.

Toward the end of August the expedition struck good water at Sweetwater Creek and followed it for several miles. Then the colonel turned back and worked his way toward the supply train on Otter Creek. His exhausted men and horses could not travel much farther. Many horses died, and about a dozen became so useless that Mackenzie had to turn them out on the prairie.

The expedition reached the Otter Creek camp on September 1, and Mackenzie found that some of Colonel Grierson's companies, who had been left in the field, were living in near luxury. Capt. L. L. Carpenter, Tenth Cavalry, invited Mackenzie and his field adjutant, Lieutenant Carter, to dinner. Carpenter offered a full-course meal on a table with a tablecloth and real dishes. African-American soldiers of the Tenth Cavalry served the dinner. Many had been experienced house servants on large plantations before the war, so Carpenter took advantage of their cooking skills.

As the meal progressed, Mackenzie grew more amazed that anyone would live in such luxury on a field expedition. The meal was served in several courses, including soup, fish that had been caught in a nearby stream, wild turkey, and quail. Mackenzie's face took on a look of pure astonishment as Carpenter's cook served the dessert — fresh-baked prune pie.

As he and Lieutenant Carter rode away from Carpenter's camp, Mackenzie turned to his adjutant. "Prune pie! And in the field. What do you think of that?"

Surprised that Grierson would depart so much from custom on an Indian campaign, Mackenzie also felt disgusted that Grierson's men lived in luxury in field camp while his own men became ill from constant movement and contaminated water. Grierson's men meanwhile remained in their field camp, stocking their food supply with wild game, and giving their cooks time to make prune pie.

Even more annoying was the fact that both expeditions maneuvered in the field in search of Indians that the government apparently didn't want found anyway. At least the dispatch he read from Reynolds seemed to say that. The government feared an all-out Indian war if the Native Americans were punished too severely, so they were allowed to wander on and off the reservation at will. All that the government wanted Mackenzie to do was to get the Indians back on for the time being.

As well as receiving the letter from Reynolds, which hampered Mackenzie's actions against the Indians, he also received a copy of a letter to Colonel Grierson from Agent Tatum at Fort Sill. Tatum said that Kicking Bird had brought more than forty mules — the number stolen in the Salt Creek raid — and promised to stay on the reservation. Tatum added that Grierson told Kicking Bird to hurry back onto the reservation before Mackenzie's expedition overtook him. Mackenzie's reputation as a "do something" commander was spreading. Grierson knew Mackenzie would attack Kicking Bird if he caught him off the reservation.

Disgustedly, Mackenzie put the dispatches back on the case.

In the fall campaign approved by General Reynolds, Mackenzie could take his large Fourth Cavalry command farther west into the Staked Plains. Grierson's authority as reservation commander did not extend there. If Mackenzie found any renegade Indians, he didn't intend to herd them politely back to the reservation. The scene of mutilated bodies around the wagons at Salt Creek was still clear in his mind.

Chapter Nine

Blanco Canyon Tragedies

In early October 1871, after less than a month's rest, Colonel Mackenzie led 600 men of his Fourth Cavalry and 100 pack mules westward from their supply camp on the beautiful bend of the Clear Fork of the Brazos River. The men wore their lightweight summer uniforms, many of which had faded to a light blue from numerous washings and long months of wear. The gold stripe down the leg had bleached to beige on many pants. On the warm day, typical in early October for Texas, prospects seemed good for a successful campaign, and Mackenzie and his men were in high spirits. The troopers sang merrily to their old regimental song.

"Come home, John, don't stay long; Come home soon to your own chick-a-biddy."

Mackenzie sent out his twenty Tonkawa scouts, under their cavalry leader Lt. Peter Boehm, to ride in advance of the column of marching troopers. The scouts were instructed to comb the area for signs of Indians. The Tonkawas were peaceful Texas Indians who bitterly hated their enemies, the Comanches. They served the white man faithfully as scouts in order to fight Comanches.

Two days later, Mackenzie led his men through an immense herd of plodding buffalo. He cautioned the men not to shoot any of the shaggy beasts because the noise would reveal the Army's presence to the Indians. Even more tempting to his men were antelope that scampered along the edge of the huge buffalo herd. Troopers guided their horses among the moving sea of buffaloes, while fussing at the slower pace, the dust in their faces, and the orders not to hunt.

The command clearly traveled in Indian country, the Panhandle of Texas. Spanish-speaking Indians called it Llano Estacado, the Staked Plains, because it appeared that something held up the plains hundreds of feet higher than the land to the southeast.

On October 9, Mackenzie ordered the command to camp in Blanco Canyon. Shortly after midnight, the men were awakened by yelling and the sound of stampeding horses. A milling confusion centered near the area of the camp where the cavalry horses grazed. No doubt existed this time as to whether or not the Indians had started the stampede. Kwahadi Comanches rode bareback at full speed through camp, yelling, shaking dried buffalo robes, and ringing bells. Troopers fired wildly at the dim, fast-moving forms, and men grabbed for their own mounts to keep from losing them. Colonel Mackenzie yelled orders to hold on to as many horses as possible, but his men acted too late to retrieve them all.

In his nervousness at the unexpected Indian attack, Mackenzie unconsciously rubbed together the stumps of his two amputated fingers. The Indians would soon begin to call him "Bad Hand" because of the missing fingers on his right hand. This name may have meant even more, for the arrival of Ranald Mackenzie on the frontier was "bad" for the Indians raiding there.

Within twenty minutes the confusion died down, and the camp became orderly again as the Indians drove the horses away from camp. Mackenzie ordered a count to see how many horses the Indians had taken. He learned that they had stolen about seventy horses, including his own prized gray pacer. The colonel knew that it would be useless to chase the Indians in the blackness. The Comanches knew the country well, while he did not, and his men could easily be ambushed. He went back to his blanket to try to sleep.

Before dawn he awoke and called in Lieutenant Carter. He sent the lieutenant and a detail of twelve men to search for some of the horses that might have strayed away from the Indians or become lost from the herd during the stampede.

A few minutes after Carter and his men left, Mackenzie and the troopers in camp heard several shots. Knowing that the detachment had encountered Indians, Mackenzie ordered the remainder of the command to mount up. He led them in the direction of the firing. They arrived in time to finish the fight between Carter's small detail and about a hundred Indians who had trapped them in a box canyon. The Indians' arrows killed Pvt. Seander Gregg. Carter's horse took an arrow and fell on its rider, shattering the lieutenant's right leg.

The Comanches fled up the canyon into bluffs and boulders along its walls, where they shot at the troopers for a while. Gradually, they disappeared over the rim onto the Llano Estacado.

Mackenzie realized that his tired horses could not overtake the fleeing Indians. Like the soldiers, the horses were weakened by bad water and short rations on the field expedition. Some of Mackenzie's best horses were in Comanche hands, and others were worn out from the stampede of the previous night. So Mackenzie led his men back down into the valley, where he directed the burial of Private Gregg. He sent his Tonkawa scouts to follow the trail of the Comanches.

About midafternoon the scouts returned with a report that they had found a trail that they believed led to the Comanche village. Mackenzie started his men in pursuit, but realizing their exhaustion, he led them only a few miles before camping for the night. This time the colonel took more precautions to keep the Indians from stampeding his remaining horses. He ordered the horses hobbled, as he had done the night before, but he also stationed parties of men to stay through the night with the herd. Early the following morning, Mackenzie ordered the men who had lost their mounts in the stampede to return to the supply camp.

Mackenzie offered to detail Lieutenant Carter in command of the unmounted soldiers returning to supply camp so that the young lieutenant could relieve his shattered leg. However, Carter preferred to remain with the column of mounted troopers.

Mackenzie then led the rest of his men along the bank of the White River, which flowed at the bottom of Blanco Canyon. Late that afternoon they reached the site of the Indian village, which the Comanches had hastily abandoned only a short time earlier.

The command camped there for the night. The next morning Mackenzie led his command along the trail that the Comanches cleverly left to confuse them. The trail divided and then crossed and recrossed the river in every direction.

The colonel depended entirely on his Tonkawa scouts. They lost and then found the real trail several times, but by afternoon they knew that they were gaining on the Comanches because of the increasing number of items discarded along the trail as the Indians hurried to stay ahead of the cavalry. They dropped lodge poles and skins, stone hammers, wood, and even half-wolf puppies. Some of the soldiers picked up the little animals and carried them on the knobs of their saddles.

The land on which the men rode remained a level plain with few trees in sight, but its elevation gradually seemed to become higher than the land on which they had ridden in previous days. Also the air seemed cooler.

Mackenzie began to notice a few Indian warriors from time to time at the sides of his column of troopers, and he received reports that Comanches had also been sighted at the rear of the command. The Indians apparently were trying to delay his advance. He instructed the cavalry to ride on all four sides of the pack mules to keep them from being stampeded.

Late that afternoon, dark clouds formed. Soon a drizzle drifted down on them, making visibility difficult. Then the moisture turned to sleet and snow. Mackenzie and his men pulled their light summer uniforms closer around them and kept moving. Those who were fortunate enough to carry blankets or coats with them wrapped themselves and urged their horses forward.

As they topped a sudden ridge, Mackenzie dimly saw hundreds of moving forms — the Comanche village! The Indians were milling about in their confusion and haste at trying to get away.

The wind became stronger, swirling the snow and sleet around them in blinding gusts. The men could not see far in front of them and only maintained the marching column by riding very close behind each other.

The colonel was forced to order his command to halt and dismount so that blankets on the pack animals could be distributed among the freezing men. He sent Capt. Wint Davis and a detachment in pursuit of the Indians. A few warriors charged Davis' column and then disappeared into the darkness.

Some of the officers angrily asked Mackenzie why he hadn't ordered an attack on the village. The reasons were simple, though infuriating. The freezing and exhausted men had been able to see clearly only a few feet in front of them. The supply camp lay a hundred miles away. If he had ordered an attack, the men would have milled around and fired at each other. The entire command, which was under his sole responsibility, might have been scattered or destroyed in the freezing snowstorm.

Mackenzie had been within firing distance of an entire Comanche village living illegally off the reservation, and all he could do was sit still and let them get away. He told the men to unpack tarpaulins, robes, and blankets and try to get warm.

Soon Captain Davis reported that the darkness made it impossible to see the Indians. He and his men had managed to find their way back to camp in the blinding snow by yelling back and forth with the Tonkawas to keep the location of the command clear.

Mackenzie knew he had made the right decision in not attacking the Indians. It might have been a massacre for most of his men. The Comanches knew the terrain better than his command. Yet many of Mackenzie's men probably did not understand all the reasons for not attacking. The disgruntled cavalrymen, huddled around campfires that October night trying to get warm, were in a far different mood than they had been earlier in the month when they had begun their expedition. The men shivered around the campfires in their blankets and tried to get warm enough to go to sleep.

The next day dawned clear and beautiful, though cold. The snow covered all signs of the Comanches, who evidently had gotten far ahead by traveling all night in the storm.

The colonel knew that the spirit of the men in the command was sagging. Also, many of the animals seemed on the verge of dropping. Water in the canteens was low, and no firewood remained. Mackenzie ordered his men to turn back toward the supply camp. Along the way they picked up a few long poles used by the Comanches to prop up their lodges. In their haste the Indians had discarded them. The poles made excellent firewood for the soldiers.

A day later, as they descended Blanco Canyon, the Tonkawa scouts found two Comanche braves at the edge of the column of troopers. The scouts chased the Comanches to a bushy ravine along the wall of the canyon. Mackenzie ordered Lieutenant Boehm to take fifteen men on foot to drive the two Indians from cover. The Comanches fired arrows at the detail as the entire command watched. Impatient to capture the two Indians so

47

that his weeks in the field would not be wasted entirely, Mackenzie rode up to watch Boehm and his Tonkawas. One of the Comanches shot an arrow that imbedded itself in Mackenzie's right thigh, all the way to the bone. Soon bullets from Boehm's scouts ended the lives of the two Comanches.

Soldiers rushed up and carried Mackenzie to the surgeon at the rear of the column. He seemed embarrassed at all the fuss made over him, and the wound seemed more of a disgrace because there had not even been a battle.

He ordered the command into camp and moved unhurriedly the next day to the mouth of the canyon where the quartermaster, 1st Lt. Henry Lawton, arrived from supply camp with his welcome wagons of supplies and forage for the animals.

Mackenzie's wound in his right thigh made riding extremely painful. At camp, after relinquishing command to his senior officer, Capt. Clarence Mauch, he refused to stay quietly in his tent as the doctor had ordered. Because of his many wounds suffered during the Civil War, and then the thigh injury, Mackenzie's weak frame suffered pain much of the time anyway. He often became nervous and irritable, particularly on a field expedition when he ran the risk of complete defeat at the hands of a large body of Indians. The fact that the sole responsibility for the safety of his command of several hundred men rested entirely with him contributed to his nervous state of mind. The men respected Mackenzie because he was a bold, daring leader, but they sometimes grew tired of his irritable nature because they did not understand what caused it. One of these times came at the field camp on Duck Creek. Some of the men had put the doctor up to a little teasing of the colonel, to hint to him that he should control his temper a little better.

Dr. Gregory, the field surgeon, cornered Mackenzie and led him to his tent, telling him he had to examine his injured leg. When Mackenzie inquired how it was doing, the doctor replied, "Sir, the condition of it is so bad that if you don't control your temper and maintain absolute quiet, I'll have to amputate."

Yelling that no one was going to amputate his leg, Mackenzie grabbed his crutch and ordered the doctor out of his tent. Only then did he hear the doctor and the men outside laughing. In his pain and frustration of having his expedition hampered, Mackenzie didn't think the joke very funny.

Captain Mauch and the command arrived in camp a few days later in a freezing snowstorm. Many of the cavalry horses had died due to severe weather conditions and exhaustion.

Another field expedition — an unsuccessful one — had ended. Mackenzie had lost many horses; several men had sustained wounds, including Mackenzie; one man had died; and the Comanches had remained unpunished. Of course, the young colonel did gain a little more information about the Comanches' hideouts in the Llano Estacado and the tricks they used in fighting. He would use this information later. The stamina shown by the Comanches in traveling with their entire village during the blinding storm revealed them as an adversary to be respected. Ranald Mackenzie was developing into a cavalry leader to be respected as well.

Henry Strong, the young adventurer who rode to Weatherford after Henry Warren in May, had attached himself to Mackenzie's summer expedition. The young bachelor owned a ranch in Jack County but seemed free to seek adventure whenever he pleased. Around Christmastime he invited Mackenzie and two other new army friends to his ranch northwest of Jacksboro for a hunting trip. Strong, Mackenzie, and Lieutenants Will Thompson and Henry Lawton pitched camp at Cambron Creek. The creek was named after the Cambron family, who had been killed by Indians.

Though the men had only two shotguns between them, they filled two wagons with wild turkeys and sent them back to the fort for the men. They killed bear and even went after a panther that threatened the camp one night. Strong found a fresh trail of Indians leading seven horses, which changed the object of the hunt from animal to human game. The men feared that a trail of stolen horses, scalpings, and burned cabins lay behind the Comanches, so they hurried back to Fort Richardson after losing the Indians' tracks.

Because of Strong's ability to find Indians, Mackenzie offered him a job as army scout in the Fourth Cavalry.

"I don't think it pays very much — only about a thousand a year," the colonel said apologetically. To hog rancher Strong, who was in debt for $85 and whose animals had scattered, the sum seemed quite enough, so he accepted readily.

Thus, at every opportunity Mackenzie prepared his command for further field expeditions against raiding Indians, adding more scouts with skilled knowledge of the country. His chances for success against the Indians were mounting steadily.

Chapter Ten

Comanchero Trail

R anald Mackenzie became greatly pleased early in 1872 upon learning that Gen. C. C. Augur had replaced Gen. J. J. Reynolds as commander of the Department of Texas. Mackenzie liked his new superior officer much better than he liked Reynolds.

The Army had finally agreed that the frontier situation should be placed under the charge of a man who believed in letting the cavalry get out and deal with hostile Indians rather than waste time sitting around the various posts. Mackenzie knew that now he would get more support for his campaign against the rebelling Kiowas and Comanches than he had gotten from Reynolds.

A bit of bad feeling had developed between Mackenzie and his former commander late in 1871. Either through oversight or in an attempt to hurry the start of his field campaign, Mackenzie failed to follow through on some red-tape regulations in requesting provisions for his command. Reynolds began court-martial proceedings against the colonel for not buying from the approved contractors. Mackenzie, in turn, honestly felt that Reynolds dipped his hand into government money by taking "kickbacks" from these contractors who provided shoddy provisions, so the colonel accused his superior of fraud. A great deal of dishonesty did exist among some of the officers of the U.S. Army. When all of it came to light about four years later, the military received much criticism for scandals within the department. High-ranking officers like Reynolds, if guilty, were exposed.

Early hints to Reynolds' participation in the frauds may have influenced his replacement by Augur. The court-martial proceedings were dropped. Mackenzie happily welcomed Augur as his new superior, and the two men readily agreed on another field expedition for June of that year.

During the spring, while preparations continued, Mackenzie served on a court-martial at Fort Richardson in February and one at Fort Sill in March, where he sat as president of the court-martial. Such duties irritated the colonel, for Indian raids continued in the vicinity of the ranches and farms surrounding his command post, Fort Richardson. While he was away at Fort Sill, Indians raided near Weatherford, only forty miles from Fort Richardson. Citizens of the area did not understand Army regulations requiring Mackenzie's presence in Fort Sill, and they complained that Indians were allowed to approach too near the fort.

Down in southern Texas, out of Mackenzie's area of responsibility, Indians with whom he would come in contact later in the year had carried out a large raid. Sixty Kiowas and Comanches, seven Mexicans, and six or eight African-American deserters from the United States Army led by Big Bow attacked a train of wagons and sixteen whites on April 20, 1872. The scene of the attack where Indians burned nine Texans alive was Howard's Wells, located above Fort Clark in Crockett County. Some people referred to the Howard's Wells attack as "another Salt Creek Massacre." Actually, it revealed more cruelty than the raid a year earlier at Salt Creek Prairie.

In mid-May, Colonel Mackenzie sent 2nd Lt. John A.

McKinney, scout Henry Strong, and ten men after about twenty Indians who raided in Jack County. They caught up with them near the falls on the Big Wichita River, and a skirmish took place. The Indians escaped, and the troopers did not obtain an account of the number killed. They definitely saw the Indians pick up three of their fallen braves.

Also in May, the colonel traveled to San Antonio to confer personally with General Augur about his early summer expedition. The little Spanish city in southern Texas was a place of memories for Ranald Mackenzie. Florida Tunstall, now Mrs. Redford Sharpe, still made her home in San Antonio and now had a child. Mackenzie's visit to San Antonio was on Army business, however, and he did not have time to visit Florida and her family.

The proposed field expedition planned to put an end to the illegal trade among three groups: Indians who left their reservations to raid in Texas, those who had never allowed themselves to be moved to a reservation; and outlaw Mexicans. This trade had continued in one way or another for more than a hundred years among the Spaniards, Indians, and Mexicans.

The Mexicans, some of whom were half-breeds, as well as the white men who participated in the illegal trade, acquired the name "Comancheros." Sometimes poor Mexicans brought only a few burro loads of trade goods to the rendezvous, while rich Mexicans hauled many wagon loads of products to trade with the Indians. Most Comancheros, wealthy or not, desired one thing — cattle. Occasionally, the poor Mexicans obtained only ten or twenty head for their few trade items, while the wealthy Comancheros drove away herds of as many as 500 cattle. The Indians obtained the cattle for trading to the Comancheros by stealing from farmers or ranchers on the northern Texas frontier.

Augur intended to have Mackenzie stop this trade. Part of the trade goods the Mexicans furnished the Indians in exchange for cattle consisted of guns, ammunition, whiskey, tobacco, hardtack, sugar, coffee, arrows, and spear points. Sometimes the Comancheros accepted white captives for their goods instead of cattle. These they sold to the captives' white relatives at outrageous prices. Some Mexican citizens of San Antonio had even been captured by the renegade Indians for trade to the Comancheros.

Some of the Indians involved in the illegal trade comprised the Kwahadi and Kotsoteka Comanche bands who refused to abide by the 1867 Treaty of Medicine Lodge by failing to accept reservation life. Those living illegally in the Texas Panhandle at this time totaled 1,500. One of the Kotsoteka chiefs, Mow-way, explained, "When the Indians on the reservations are better treated than we are outside, it will be time enough to come in."

Mackenzie could understand Mow-way's reasoning. This was why the colonel protested so vigorously that dishonest contractors should not cheat the reservation Indians out of their proper supplies. Such dishonest dealings made it even more difficult to keep the Indians on the reservation. Often they went hungry for lack of supplies, while the renegade Indians off the reservation became rich from plundering frontier farms and ranches and from trading with the Mexican Comancheros.

Some of the Kwahadi chiefs told Kiowa Agent Lawrie Tatum many times that they would not live on the reservation until the soldiers forced them. They refused to accept the government supplies because they could get all they needed from the Comancheros with whom they traded regularly.

Kwahadi in the Comanche language is a word meaning "runaway." The Kwahadi Comanches constituted a bad influence on the reservation Indians, ridiculing them for staying on the reservation when they could roam free and raid without being punished for being off the reservation. Consequently, the Kwahadis persuaded many Indians to leave the reservation to steal from the Texans and trade with Comancheros.

Texas frontiersmen were irritated considerably by the fact that some of the Indians who carried out the

54

plundering and murdering raids were fed, clothed, and provided with ammunition by the federal government upon the reservation in Indian Territory. The government, however, supported Grant's Quaker Peace Policy, which unsuccessfully tried to maintain the Indians on the reservations with dedicated men of the Quaker faith. Augur and Mackenzie did not agree with the unpeaceful peace policy, but had to endure it because it was the policy of both the government and the president they had sworn to serve. They just had to do the best they could in spite of the policy. Therefore, at their May meeting in San Antonio, General Augur told Colonel Mackenzie to establish a supply camp on the headwaters of the Colorado River or the Freshwater Fork of the Brazos and to scout westward in territory never before explored by the United States Army.

Mackenzie planned to take along a half-breed captive named Polonis Ortiz, who had been captured in March near Fort Concho. Ortiz confessed that he was a Comanchero engaged in illegal trade with the Indians. He agreed to lead the cavalry along a wagon road that crossed the Llano Estacado. He said sufficient water and grass existed and that all the stolen cattle were driven over this thoroughfare to New Mexico.

Following the conference with General Augur, Mackenzie reported back to Fort Richardson. There he busied himself with the time-consuming organizational activity and paperwork necessary to prepare for field maneuvers. The upcoming expedition would be his largest yet, and he planned to remain in the field longer than on any of his three previous expeditions the year before.

He would operate out of Fort Griffin, with that place as his supply base, although another supply camp would be set up farther out in the field. The command would total six cavalry companies, four infantry companies, and more than thirty-two wagons. For this large command he needed a great many supplies because he planned to remain in the field four months.

In June, Mackenzie wrote a letter to his army superiors, protesting against the Quaker Peace Policy. He wrote, "Indian depredations are becoming alarmingly frequent, and the depredators are Kiowas and Comanches who are fed daily by the Indian agent on the Canadian River." Gen. Philip Sheridan, both Mackenzie's and Augur's superior, agreed. He endorsed Mackenzie's letter and said it seemed senseless to try to protect the frontier of northern Texas from Indians who obtained food, arms, and ammunition from the agent on the reservation. Thus the military men regarded the peace policy of Grant as a failure. The problem, however, was to make this clear both to Grant and to the Interior Department, which administered the policy.

As Mackenzie, his scouts, and a small escort traveled to Fort Griffin for the Big Scout, as the settlers called it, Lt. Richard Taylor met them seven miles out from the fort. He told of a recent raid on a family named Lee, who lived fifteen miles below Fort Griffin. Renegades had murdered, scalped, and horribly mutilated four members of the family and had kidnapped two girls, ages eighteen and sixteen, and a boy, ten. The eighteen-year-old girl, raised on the frontier, escaped from the Indians the first night and followed a back trail by moonlight. The next night she encountered Mackenzie's force. She hid in a washed-out gully for a time, thinking they were Indians. Finally, she came toward the soldiers and threw up her hands with joy. Mackenzie sent her to Fort Griffin with an escort. Her brother and sister were rescued from the Indians several months later.

Mackenzie arrived at Fort Griffin on June 16 to start the field expedition. Within the next two weeks he set up his permanent field supply camp near the mouth of Blanco Canyon on the Freshwater Fork of the Brazos River. Then he divided the command into two parts. He ordered Maj. E. A. Latimer on June 28 to take two companies of men and proceed slowly to the Freshwater Fork. Mackenzie himself led two other companies to the head of Duck Creek. There they came upon a group of Comanches in camp. The Indians eluded the scouts in a long chase at dusk. Mackenzie then crossed the table-land to Blanco Canyon and proceeded down the Freshwater Fork until he met Latimer's command on July 1.

Any day, Mackenzie expected the arrival of two other companies under the command of Lt. Col. William R. Shafter, the officer who had served under him several years earlier with the Forty-first Infantry. Shafter was serving with the Fourth Cavalry. With Shafter's troops Mackenzie wanted to trap some Indians between the three sections of his command. Shafter's official arrival time — July 1 — had passed, and the walrus-mustached officer and his men had still not arrived.

Mackenzie waited — and fumed. He sent a small body of troops to scout the country while awaiting Shafter. Six days later, the missing lieutenant colonel and his men arrived in camp. Mackenzie demanded to know what had kept them.

While making plans to join Mackenzie's summer expedition, Colonel Shafter had heard that Mackenzie and some of his men had been ambushed by Indians. Shafter had sent a courier to headquarters at San Antonio to ask whether or not to proceed to the Freshwater Fork as planned. This delayed him the six days.

It seemed strange to Mackenzie to hear reports of his own death and to read accounts of it in the Texas newspaper brought by Shafter. Several Texas newspapers, which relied on hearsay for a great deal of their news, carried the story of Mackenzie's death and also a correction a few days later. A rancher named Loescher, who spread the story, had been mistaken. Writers praised the colonel, thinking they were writing his obituary:

To the frontier counties the death of General Mackenzie will prove a great loss, since he was one of the bravest and most energetic Indian fighters in the army. He was on his way back to take command of the great expedition which it is understood is being inaugurated at

57

the upper forts against the Indians and his untimely death will materially interfere with its success, it is feared. The surprise happened between Fort Belknap and Jacksboro where Mr. Loescher witnessed the whole affair, about 300 yards distant, hidden from view by the bushes.

Newspaper articles generally referred to Colonel Mackenzie as a general because of the honorary rank to which he had risen in the Civil War. Writers praised him as an energetic Indian fighter, although he had not yet actually succeeded in engaging the Native Americans in a large battle. At least he had gone out looking for those who were perpetrating raids, which was more than most other post commanders in the state had done. Some of his men, too, had skirmished with Indians during scouting forays in past years.

Before taking out his entire command, Mackenzie still had to wait for the men he had sent out before Shafter arrived. While waiting for them to return, he led a detachment on a two-week scouting foray. Finally, late in July, he led his entire command westward.

Soon after starting, he ordered Polonis Ortiz, the half-breed prisoner, brought to him for questioning. Mackenzie asked Ortiz to lead the command to Mucha Que Hill, where the man claimed some of the illegal trading took place. The dark man, who possessed some Comanche blood, agreed that he would.

During the next several days Mackenzie led his command deeper onto the Staked Plains, or Llano Estacado as Ortiz called the high plains located in the Texas Panhandle. Soon Mackenzie's scouts reported many Indian tracks in the area. He followed several at Ortiz's direction, but found no renegades. Numerous scattered trails departed from the main one. Even the big trail that Mackenzie followed for a time broke into several smaller ones going in all directions. By this time Mackenzie and his men had entered New Mexico Territory and had proceeded toward Fort Sumner. Mackenzie headed for that post to rest his men and horses, obtain supplies, and get information.

Several days later, after resting the men, he returned to Texas by a different route across the Staked Plains in hopes of coming upon the Comancheros. Near the head of Palo Duro Creek his men found Indians and followed them a few miles, but scouts reported that they simply constituted a small party a long way from home. Mackenzie sought the entire Indian village that had escaped him the autumn before in the blinding snowstorm.

The colonel sent his cavalry down the Palo Duro Canyon, but the main body of his command, including the infantry guarding the supplies, returned to the wagon road that Ortiz had pointed out.

By the end of August the command reached their first campsite of the expedition near Blanco Canyon. Mackenzie wrote a report to his superior, General Augur, about his summer activities: "In one month I traversed the Staked Plains twice by different routes in an area never before officially explored. I regret, however, that I traveled so far without intercepting the Comancheros."

General Augur recognized the amount of effort put into the four-month-long summer expedition and seemed pleased with Mackenzie's work, even though the colonel had not engaged any Indians in a battle. The general even sent a report to Washington stating his feelings: "This fact, that troops can be so moved, and the general knowledge of the route and operations of the cattle thieves, obtained by Colonel Mackenzie, I regard as very important, and well worth the summer's labor. Maps and itineraries are being prepared by him and will be completed when his command comes in."

Even before his summer expedition ended, Mackenzie made plans for a fall expedition in the same area. He believed that relentless campaigning, characteristic of his former service on the Texas frontier, would soon result in success. The Comanches under Mow-way or Quanah Parker could not elude him forever. He hoped that the fall campaign, which was just a month away, would reveal a turning point in his luck.

Chapter Eleven

Fight at McClellan's Creek

When Col. Ranald Mackenzie rode at the head of his double column of blue-coated troopers one late September day, he did not know that the afternoon's events would cause repercussions on the Comanche-Kiowa reservation and even in Washington, D.C. He and his Tonkawa scouts led the cavalry command alongside McClellan's Creek, located in the southeastern edge of the Texas Panhandle. The warm sun had reached its noontime peak an hour earlier and was now traveling westward in the same direction as the command. Mackenzie seemed to be in the field a great deal lately. His expedition to New Mexico had concluded only a month earlier.

Mackenzie looked up to find two of his Tonkawa scouts riding toward him rapidly. They reported finding fresh tracks leading downstream. The men in line behind their colonel became excited at the report that Indians might be nearby. Most of the men were the same ones who had been on the colonel's three previous expeditions, and they were nearly as anxious as their commander to contact the wary Comanches.

The colonel sent the Tonkawas back to follow the

trail and kept the command close behind, hoping to encounter the Comanches at any time. For nearly an hour they followed the fresh trail. Suddenly, the men saw the scouts returning through some timber along the banks of McClellan's Creek. Another wave of excitement engulfed the command. Surely the scouts must have sighted the village and were returning to warn the men to prepare for the attack. Many of the younger recruits expressed fear of the approaching battle, now that it seemed only moments away.

The men in the command might just as well have been less afraid because the scouts merely reported that they had lost the trails of the Comanches. Two trails existed, they said — one of two horses, and one of a mule — and the scouts had lost them both. Indian fighting or tracking seemed to be a series of frustrations. This was just one more added to the list that Colonel Mackenzie had learned to endure. He halted the command. There was no point in moving forward when the fresh tracks meant that the Indians were camped nearby. If the command moved, they might move away from the Indians. He instructed the scouts to go back and locate the tracks again while the troopers waited.

Capt. Wint Davis rode up to Mackenzie asking permission to go with the scouts. He reported that he had done a little scouting during the war and wanted to help now. Mackenzie told him to go ahead, but not to get out of sight of the command.

A few minutes later, Davis and the scouts rode back excitedly. They had found the tracks. Davis explained that he had noticed grapevines along the banks of the creek and had stopped to check for signs of Indians known to favor the wild fruit. He had found mule tracks, as well as trampled grapes scattered about. The Comanches apparently had used the mule to carry the grapes to their village. This meant that the Indian encampment, including the women and children, could not be very far away.

Davis and the scouts led the column along the newly

61

discovered trail, and the column of 250 troopers closed up ranks and followed closely behind. At any minute Mackenzie was expecting the scouts to ride back and report the sighting of the village. But more than an hour passed with no word. The moving column of troopers had covered twelve miles since leaving the grapevines.

Finally, the scouts stopped at the top of a rise. Mackenzie halted his command of blue uniformed soldiers who marched two by two, and a few of the men detached themselves and rode up beside the scouts. Below, three or four miles away, lay a large Indian village in a beautiful valley. Trees grew in a twisting line to the side of the village, indicating that a little creek trickled between the rows of multicolored trees.

The scouts estimated to Mackenzie that the village probably contained between 200 and 300 lodges, representing nearly 500 Native American men able to do combat. Mackenzie's command totaled 231 cavalrymen. Although his entire expedition, which had left Fort Griffin two weeks earlier, totaled nearly that many more, the rest remained with the supply wagons many miles back. The odds in this long-awaited encounter would therefore be two to one against the soldiers of the Fourth Cavalry.

Mackenzie instructed his men to dismount and refresh themselves from nearby McClellan's Creek. Older soldiers who had fought Indians before began giving quick advice to the younger recruits to keep their heads and not panic. Mackenzie called in his captains to give them their instructions.

Excitement within the command reached a new high, but the tension that had mounted during the twelve-mile ride seemed to be replaced by a certain calmness inspired by the older officers' confidence in their commander and by Mackenzie's quick instructions, which indicated his control of the situation. He rapidly outlined a plan for half of the command to surround the village and to go after the horse herd, while the rest of the men charged through the center of the village.

After receiving their instructions, the cavalrymen formed in companies ready to charge. Capt. Eugene B. Beaumont's Troop A lined up two abreast. Davis' Company F fell in beside Troop A, which made the men four abreast. The other companies also lined up four abreast.

The sun had already traveled two-thirds of the way toward its goal on the western horizon by the time Mackenzie motioned for the men to charge. His watch showed 4:00 P.M.

Mackenzie led his men at a fast gallop toward the Indian village. Three miles away, the Indians seemed like tiny moving specks as they drove hundreds of horses toward their village. They remained unaware of the cavalry charge because no bugles had yet been sounded.

When the blue-coated cavalrymen came within one-half mile of the village, the Indians saw them and began to panic. Women screamed and children began to wail as the frightened Comanches scampered to the lodges or to other cover. Some ran for their horses, while others tried to hide in the bushes and ravines surrounding their camp. The trees along the creek provided cover for the fleeing women and children. The braves and some of the women grabbed weapons to defend their lodges, and shots soon rang out on the open prairie. Finally, a cavalry bugle sounded.

Following Mackenzie's instructions, Captain Lee and his D Company began to round up the large horse herd. Company I, commanded by Capt. N. B. McLaughlin, charged through some lodges that were detached from the main village. Then Mackenzie himself led the remainder of his command in a charge through the main camp. The sound of gunshots and screaming women and children filled the air. Officers yelled instructions to their men, especially to the younger enlisted men who were participating in their first encounter with the red man. Mackenzie yelled instructions, telling men to move from a dangerous position or to head off some fleeing Indians.

The Comanches tried to rescue the body of each Indian who fell because they believed that a dead warrior could not enter the spiritual world if he were scalped or mutilated. Since the Indians scalped and mutilated the bodies of their enemies, red or white, they assumed that the white man would do the same. Of course, Indian scouts usually rode with army commands, and the scouts often did scalp their enemies.

As the charging cavalrymen reached the center of the circle of lodges, several Comanches appeared from some waist-high grass fifteen feet away where they had crouched unnoticed during the main attack. Company F, under Captain Davis, rode past the tall grass. The Comanches directed a hail of bullets and arrows at the luckless men, and four troopers fell.

Heavy firing continued for more than thirty minutes as the troopers charged through the village, emptying their guns at fleeing Indians. Then the village surrendered. Women and children came out of tepees with their hands held high.

Mackenzie sent McLaughlin and Davis with their companies after those Comanches who were still fleeing beyond the outskirts of the village. He ordered Beaumont and Lee to round up the scattered ponies.

The Tonkawas who served as scouts for Mackenzie began scalping the fallen Comanches. When informed of the actions of the Tonkawas, Mackenzie immediately made them stop their brutal rites.

Many minutes elapsed before an accurate report of casualties could be obtained. Mackenzie learned that one soldier lay dead and three suffered serious wounds — the four ambushed men of Davis' company. Troopers found twenty-three dead Comanches. Others had probably died and were carried away by the escaping Indians. McLaughlin reported capturing 124 women and children.

Mackenzie then ordered that the Comanche village be burned. Lacking food and other supplies, the Indians would be forced to return to the reservation where they were assigned.

Thus, when fate finally allowed Mackenzie to encounter the proud Comanches in their own element — the unsettled area of western Texas — the bold colonel was able to prove to them that he was a warrior of equally tough mettle.

Chapter Twelve

After the Battle

C aptain Lee and his men rounded up the horse herd and reported that it numbered more than 1,000 animals. Some troopers guessed that the herd might even contain as many as 3,000 ponies.

Soon after the horse herd had been rounded up, a private named Jose Carrion asked to speak to Colonel Mackenzie. Carrion, a newly recruited Mexican trooper of Company A, said that he had been a teamster a few months before joining the cavalry. He reported that about forty mules captured from the Indians wore the brand belonging to the wagon master of the train that had been massacred by Indians at Howard's Wells the previous spring. Thus Mackenzie learned that he had finally clashed with those who had carried out some of the raids against the frontier citizens.

Mackenzie moved his command two miles upstream from the battle site to get away from the smoke of the smouldering village before ordering the men to go into camp for the night.

He sent Lieutenant Boehm and his Tonkawa scouts

to guard the captured Indian ponies in a little gully about a mile from the village. Mackenzie believed that they would be easier to hold there in case the escaped Indians returned and tried to stampede them.

During the night, a band of Comanches, shrieking their blood-curdling screams, circled the main camp of the command and fired wildly into the air. But they failed to stampede the cavalry horses, which had been carefully staked out, and the Indians disappeared from the camp.

Sounds carry for a long distance on the open prairie. Soon the unmistakable thundering of a horse stampede came from the direction of the gully where Boehm and the Tonkawas guarded the Indian herd. The Comanches had located their own captive ponies in the ravine, and Boehm and his men had not been able to prevent the Indians from regaining their mounts.

Mackenzie regretted considerably the loss of the horses. The impact of his first victory over the Indians would be considerably lessened by the loss of the entire herd. The Indians had stampeded his horses during an earlier field expedition. After that stampede and this one, Mackenzie became determined to prevent any others.

The colonel soon broke up his field command and sent his men back to their various Texas posts. He detailed troopers to escort the Comanche captives to Fort Concho in south central Texas, where facilities existed to confine them properly.

Mackenzie quickly sent reports to his superiors about his victory. Though frontier posts lacked telegraph equipment in 1872, interior towns and army headquarters at San Antonio did possess telegraph wires that could send news of the victory to Washington.

In that city, officials in the Indian Department found just the weapon they needed to bring some stubborn old chiefs to terms when they learned of Mackenzie's September 29 victory at McClellan's Creek. Conditions among reservation Indians had worsened in the summer and fall of 1872. Raids continued into Texas, particularly while Mackenzie led his scouting expedition in the Staked Plains of Texas and New Mexico. The Kiowas and Comanches had waited until he moved westward and had then attacked the frontier farms and ranches right behind his back.

Kiowa chiefs like Lone Wolf threatened that the Kiowas would not make peace or return any white captives until the government freed Chiefs Satanta and Big Tree, both of whom remained in the Texas prison at Huntsville. Lone Wolf also insisted that raids would not cease until the government extended the Indian reservation from the Rio Grande to the Missouri River. Since such an arrangement would include nearly all of the present states of Texas, New Mexico, Oklahoma, Kansas, and Nebraska, there was little likelihood that the federal government would agree to Lone Wolf's demands.

Officials suggested the need for a council and believed it would seem more important if a delegation of representatives of every tribe came to Washington for a conference in September and October of 1872. Once the delegation of chiefs reached Washington, the conference began. After much bargaining, the Washington officials at last offered what they said were their final terms. They promised to release Satanta and Big Tree the following March if the southern tribes would: 1) remain at peace until then, 2) give up the stock they had stolen from the government, and 3) release their white or Mexican captives.

While deliberations continued, officials of the Indian Department gained knowledge of Mackenzie's victory over the Comanche village on McClellan's Creek. When the officials told the chiefs at the conference that twenty-three warriors had been killed and 124 women and children taken prisoners, the chiefs became frightened and agreed to the terms mentioned. The government then promised that if the Indians kept the three parts of their agreement, the 124 prisoners taken captive by Mackenzie also would be released in March.

When the time for release came, the Indian commissioners put the Indians off and set the time of release at June 1. The federal Indian officials freed the McClellan's Creek captives, but ran into problems after promising to secure the release of Satanta and Big Tree. A Texas court had tried and sentenced the two Kiowas, and Texas Governor Edmund J. Davis became the only person who could secure their release. Texas citizens, on the frontier particularly, petitioned their governor with hundreds of letters not to release the chiefs after hearing that the federal government intended to try to accomplish it.

Knowing that he owed his first duty to the Texans who had elected him, Davis did not want to release the Indians. After receiving continued pressure from the Indian officials in Washington and on the reservation, he finally agreed to bring the two Kiowas to a conference at Fort Sill in October 1873. These federal officials had not kept their promise to release the chiefs the previous March. Of course, the officials could not keep their promise to the Indian tribes unless Davis could be persuaded to give up Satanta and Big Tree. Unfortunately, the commissioners never had any authority to make their promise in the first place.

Davis went to the conference at Fort Sill determined to demand such stiff provisions for releasing the two Kiowa chiefs that the Indians could not possibly meet them, and he would thus not have to set Satanta and Big Tree free. But once Davis reached Fort Sill, Indian Commissioner Edward Smith convinced him that Texas possessed no legal jurisdiction over the two Indians because they were not citizens. Governor Davis finally released the two Kiowas on the condition that if either broke a parole and resumed hostile activity, he would be returned to prison to serve the remainder of a life term.

Surprisingly, the Comanches had behaved much better and ceased much of their raiding in Texas during the winter of 1872–1873 and the spring of 1873, hoping that the government would release the women and children that Colonel Mackenzie had captured at McClellan's Creek. The Kiowas behaved better to secure the release of Satanta and Big Tree.

Bands of Indians straggled into the reservation, bringing stolen horses and white or Mexican captives to exchange for their relatives. Things in northwestern Texas improved and seemed to be somewhat under control, mostly due to Mackenzie's decisive victory at McClellan's Creek. The frustrations of numerous unfruitful expeditions were forgotten in the success of the autumn campaign of 1872.

Consequently, during the spring of 1873, orders came for Mackenzie to report to Fort Clark near the southern border to confer with Gen. Philip Sheridan and Secretary of War William Belknap about a new assignment. The new task seemed of sufficient importance to bring the two prominent men on a special trip to Texas just to explain Mackenzie's orders to him personally.

The bombardment of Fredericksburg by the Army of the Potomac. From Harper's Weekly, December 27, 1862.
— Photo courtesy Denver Public Library, Western History Collection

Gen. William T. Sherman.
— Photo courtesy National
Archives, 111-BA-1674

Gen. Philip Sheridan.
— Photo courtesy National
Archives, 111-BA-1570

Hospital building at Fort Richardson.
— Photo courtesy Jack County Historical Society

72

Lt. Frank Baldwin.
— Photo courtesy Panhandle-
Plains Historical National
Archives, III-SC-80655
Museum, Canyon, Texas

*Gen. Ranald Slidell
Mackenzie in the 1870s.*
— Photo courtesy Amon Carter
Museum, No. P1967.3332

Cattle raid on the Texas border. From Harper's Weekly, January 31, 1874.
— Photo courtesy Denver Public Library, Western History Collection

A scout's report at breakfast on the plains,
by Frederick Remington.
— Photo courtesy Amon Carter Museum, Fort Worth, 227.61

Capt. Frank D. Baldwin's charge on Grey Beard's Camp
at McClellan's Creek, November 8, 1874.
— Photo courtesy Amon Carter Museum, 1510.67

75

Satank, Kiowa chief.
— Photo courtesy National
Archives, 111-SC-80655

Satanta, Kiowa chief.
— Photo courtesy National
Archives, 111-SC-80651

Big Tree, Kiowa chief.
— Photo courtesy National Archives, 111-SC-87389

Lone Wolf, Kiowa chief.
— Photo courtesy Oklahoma
Historical Society

Ouray, Uncompahgre Ute.
— Photo courtesy Smithsonian
Institution National Anthropo-
logical Archives, Bureau of
American Ethnology Collection,
Neg. 1551-a

Cheyenne Dull Knife, seated, with Little Wolf.
— Photo courtesy Smithsonian Institution National
Anthropological Archives, Bureau of American
Ethnology Collection, Neg. 270-A

Reality on the Plains. From Harper's Weekly, *July 29, 1876.*
— Photo courtesy Denver Public Library, Western History Collection

The Indian War — A Sick Soldier on a Travau.
From Harper's Weekly, *October 28, 1876.*
— Photo courtesy Denver Public Library, Western History Collection

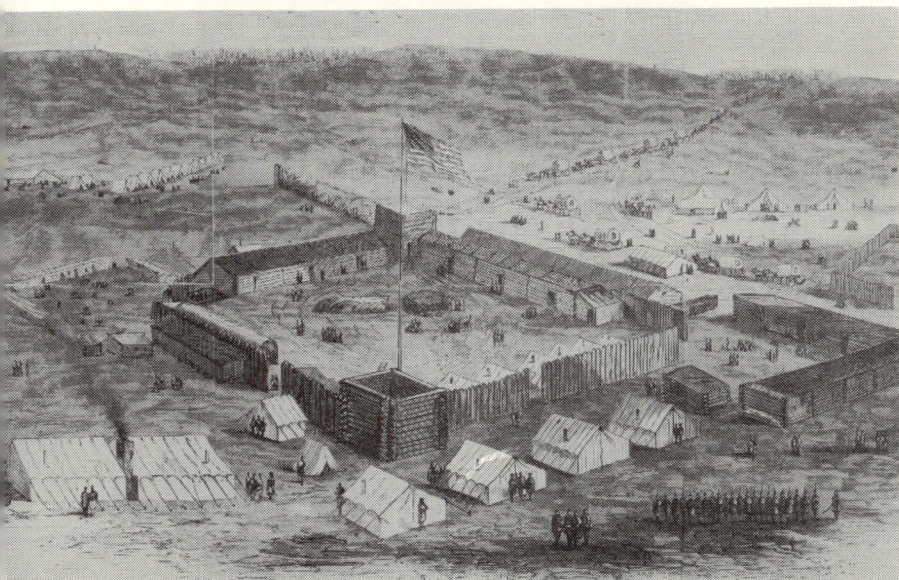

Camp Supply, Indian Territory. From Harper's Weekly.
— Photo courtesy Oklahoma Historical Society

Colorado — The late Ute outbreak and massacre at the White River Agency. The ruins after the fire and massacre. From Frank Leslie's Illustrated Newspaper, December 6, 1879.

— Photo courtesy Denver Public Library, Western History Collection

Nathan C. Meeker.
— Photo courtesy Library,
State Historical Society
of Colorado, Neg. F1314

Josephine Meeker.
— Photo courtesy Library,
State Historical Society
of Colorado, Neg. F-2577

Nelson A. Miles.
— Photo courtesy Panhandle-
Plains Historical Museum,
Canyon, Texas

Brig. Gen. George Crook.
— Photo courtesy National
Archives, 111-BA-219

Part III

To Mexico and Back: 1873–1875

Chapter Thirteen

Mackenzie's Instructions

C ol. Ranald Mackenzie sat at a table in the officers' quarters of Fort Clark with Gen. Philip Sheridan and Secretary of War William Belknap. General Sheridan told him: "Mackenzie, you have been ordered down here to relieve General Merritt and the Ninth Cavalry because I want something done to stop those conditions of banditry, killing . . . by those people across the river. I want you to control and hold down the situation, and to do it in your own way . . . I want you to be bold, enterprising and at all times full of energy. When you begin, let it be a campaign of annihilation, obliteration, and complete destruction, as you have always in your dealings done to all the Indians you have dealt with. I think you should understand what I want done, and the way you should employ your force."

Mackenzie asked Sheridan if he had any plan to suggest or if Sheridan would issue the necessary orders for Mackenzie's action. Under whose authority would Mackenzie act? Sheridan replied: "Damn the orders! Damn the authority. You are to go ahead on your own plan of action, and your authority and backing shall be General

Grant and myself. With us behind you in whatever you do to clean up this situation, you can rest assured of the fullest support. You must assume the risk. We will assume the final responsibility should any result."

The three men, two middle-aged and one youthful looking, continued talking about the unpleasant situation that had existed for many years along the Texas-Mexican border. The young colonel knew a great deal about the problem because of his years in southern Texas with the Forty-first Infantry. He was learning more.

Hostile conditions existed in the early 1870s because Mexicans and Indians raided Texas settlers on the frontier to steal their cattle. Mescalero Apaches, Lipan Apaches, and Kickapoos residing in northern Mexico crossed the Rio Grande to scalp and steal from Texas citizens living near the border. These outlaws then hastened back to the Mexican side of the river before being captured by cavalry patrols stationed at southern forts. Secretary of War Belknap had reported to President Ulysses S. Grant in 1869 that the problem loomed so great that it might have to be mentioned to the Mexican government. State Department officials made such mention and presented a request for payment for damages to Texas citizens, but the Mexican government acted slowly.

A grand jury of the United States Circuit Court for the eastern district of Texas met at Brownsville in March 1872 and reported that an average of 5,000 Texas cattle were disappearing monthly. The grand jury suggested that a properly handled mounted force, which would follow the marauders to their hideouts, could prevent such border invasions and thievery. In May a commission from the United States Congress investigated the border situation. They reported that cattle herds had shrunk to one-fourth their previous numbers, and loss of property totaled over $27 million. As a result of their investigation, the committee recommended an increase of the United States cavalry force along the southwestern frontier. Mackenzie's Fourth Cavalry, which had successfully defeated the Comanches at McClellan's Creek the previous September, seemed the most logical choice for such a responsible job.

Concerning this additional cavalry force, Gen. W. T. Sherman had written Mackenzie's immediate superior officer, General Augur: "The President wishes you to give great attention to affairs on the Rio Grande frontier, especially to prevent the raids of Indians and Mexicans upon the people and property of southern and western Texas . . . In naming the 4th for the Rio Grande the President is doubtless influenced by the fact that Col. Mackenzie is young and enterprising, and that he will impart to his regiment his own active character."

General Augur had then transferred Colonel Mackenzie to Fort Clark, where the conference with General Sheridan and Secretary of War Belknap occurred in mid-April, 1873. Mackenzie's new command post, Fort Clark, protected the ranches in Kinney County, 125 miles west of San Antonio.

Companies of the Fourth Cavalry, scattered at several frontier posts following the close of the previous summer's expedition, received orders to assemble into one large unit at Fort Clark. When all the men arrived from their various posts, Mackenzie's command totaled over 1,000 men, representing the largest unit of soldiers assembled since the close of the Civil War.

As soon as the two important visitors from Washington departed, Mackenzie ordered five companies into the field twenty miles from Fort Clark for drilling maneuvers. The men needed to be well trained and ready for any emergency for the expedition he planned. He scattered the companies of the Fourth in various directions around the post to allow the horses plenty of grazing for forage and to keep from arousing suspicion about his plans. A large force camped around the fort engaging in tactical maneuvers would have caused unwanted rumors to spread among the citizens of the little nearby town of Bracketville. Mackenzie placed two companies at each

86

campsite, except for the large Company C, which drilled alone.

For an entire month the troopers of the Fourth Cavalry engaged in target practice and charge formation. Blacksmiths shod horses; the quartermaster issued ammunition liberally to each cavalryman; and the long sabers, seldom used by cavalrymen, received extra attention as the men polished and sharpened them.

For the coming expedition, Mackenzie chose as his scouts three half-breed ranchers who had lived on the southern border for many years. He sent them across the Rio Grande, which formed the boundary between Texas and Mexico. Their task was to locate a route to the Indian villages and estimate the possible strength of the Indians.

Drilling continued throughout April and the first part of May. The men of the Fourth improved their fighting skills. Then in mid-May, Lipan Apaches and Kickapoos raided a ranch near the fort. When his scouts returned late on the night of May 16, reporting that the entire warrior force of the Kickapoo village had just ridden off toward the west, Mackenzie saw an excellent chance to retaliate for the recent raid in the vicinity. The Indian village would remain unprotected except for some old men and the women and children. It would thus be easy to capture. Such tactics seemed necessary to succeed at plains warfare.

Mackenzie sent couriers to his cavalry companies scattered in the field surrounding Fort Clark. He ordered Companies A, B, C, E, and M to meet him at Las Moras Creek as soon as possible.

By midmorning of May 17, the cavalry companies began assembling at Las Moras Creek. At noon, Company E rode in, but M still had not arrived. Mackenzie paced back and forth, impatient at the delay. An hour later, Company M rode in, stirring up the powdery dust and spreading it over the sweaty men, who were hot from their long wait in the heat of the day. Mackenzie immediately called for the command to mount up, and he led the entire column out.

His force consisted of 360 enlisted men, 17 officers, 24 scouts, and 14 private citizens who had lost cattle or loved ones to the marauders and personally wanted to assist in any retaliation against the Kickapoo and their half-breed accomplices. The colonel did not need his full-strength command of over a thousand men for the quick raid he planned. The remainder of the men patrolled various stations along the southern border or remained to protect the area around Fort Clark.

Colonel Mackenzie led his soldiers southwestward down Las Moras Creek toward the Rio Grande. Despite his earlier impatience, he maintained a leisurely course and rested the men and horses often. Because of the extremely warm spring day, he directed the men to place wet sponges in their hats to prevent a sunstroke. He planned to reach the Rio Grande at about twilight, so he gauged his speed accordingly.

Just before the men of the command guided their horses into the cool waters of the Rio Grande, Ranald Mackenzie halted the blue-uniformed troopers to explain the purpose of the expedition and their destination. He had previously revealed his plans to no one but his acting adjutant, 2nd Lt. Robert Carter. He informed the men of the dangers involved in being surprised on foreign soil and urged them to maintain absolute quiet. He stressed the need for strict compliance with orders throughout the quick raid to minimize the danger to the command.

When the men learned of their mission, a stunned silence followed. Mackenzie pressed his heels into his horse's side, turned the reins toward the river, and led his Fourth Cavalry across the Rio Grande onto alien soil in Mexico.

Chapter Fourteen

The Remolina Raid

T he mounted troopers followed their young colonel as he led his horse into the gray waters of the Rio Grande. The men welcomed the night breeze after the sweltering heat of the day. If they had any fears about the outcome of the raid, they hid them. A soldier's duty is to follow orders, and their colonel had ordered a silent crossing and a quick raid into Mexican territory.

Once across the Rio Grande, Ranald Mackenzie led his men rapidly, following the route his three scouts directed from the front of the column. They estimated the distance and knew how long it would take to reach the Kickapoo and Lipan Apache villages, more than sixty miles inside the interior of Mexico. Mackenzie wanted to reach them by daybreak for a surprise attack.

A light fog made the moving column appear ghostlike and eerie in the warm mid-May evening. The night was the kind to make a rider feel that phantom Indians or angry Mexicans might materialize out of the blackness at any moment.

Gradually, the mounted horsemen began to move more and more slowly. Mackenzie noticed it and sent word back for the column to maintain its pace. The men immediately hurried their animals and closed up the line for a time, but in a short while a gradual slackening occurred again.

The heavily laden pack mules, carrying two days' provisions for the men, could not maintain the rapid pace Mackenzie had set after crossing the Rio Grande. The mules lay down, balked, and caused their drivers to curse more than usual for one day. The tired mules slowed the entire column of mounted cavalrymen. Finally, Lieutenant Carter rode to the front and informed the colonel of the problem. Nervous because he was responsible for 300 men on foreign soil, Mackenzie consented to halt the column only five minutes to cut the packs loose and abandon them. They could be picked up on the return to Texas after the battle. He told the men to open some of the packs and distribute the hard bread. That would be their only food until the return trip.

While the men dismounted for a five-minute rest to stretch their legs, Mackenzie also dismounted and paced back and forth impatiently. Five minutes later, the colonel ordered his men to resume the rapid march. After consulting with his scouts again, he determined that with no more stops and a steady pace the command might make the village of Remolina by daybreak.

After three more hours in the saddle, Mackenzie's body ached from the strain of the fast pace. His right thigh, wounded at Blanco Canyon, began to throb severely. So did his right shoulder, in which he had suffered a wound during the Civil War. Still he did not slow the pace.

A faint glow from the east greeted the men before they reached the Remolina River. A few minutes later, Mackenzie rested the column at the river so that the cavalrymen and horses could refresh themselves before making a fast charge into the village. He ordered every man to carry his cartridges in his pockets rather than in his saddlebags, in case any trooper became separated from his horse.

The two Kickapoo villages and one Lipan Apache village stretched three miles along the south bank of the little Remolina River. The scouts suggested that Mackenzie divide his command and send half the soldiers three miles down the river to attack from that end. This would prevent the inhabitants of the Lipan village from escaping. Mackenzie cautiously refused to divide his command. Three years later, former classmate George Armstrong Custer would divide his command, and nearly 300 of his men would be killed. Custer would also fail to tell his men to carry ammunition in their pockets, as Mackenzie wisely thought to do.

Mackenzie's men began lining up in battle formation as he gave commands to his captains gathered around him. He planned to have the men charge by platoons. After delivering a volley of lead as they rode through the village, the men in the platoon would wheel out of the way of the men behind them, return to the rear, reload, and then charge again.

Mackenzie gave orders for the first group to charge, and almost immediately the quiet, sleeping village changed into a yelling, screaming mass of moving bodies, charging horses, and flying bullets. The dust kicked up by the horses as they ran through the village combined with the smoke of the shots, making it difficult to see anything.

The victorious troopers yelled wildly, galloping through the village. Gray smoke and the smell of burning grass filled the air. Rifles cracked as the well-trained troopers sent their bullets flying toward the running targets. Horses screamed and reared, with nostrils flaring.

Although the command did not reach the villages exactly by daybreak as the colonel had planned, the attack surprised the Indians completely. With the braves absent from the village, the remaining women and children scattered like frightened animals. They fled across irrigation ditches and cornfields, away from their village. Capt. N. B. McLaughlin and his men followed close behind them. The Indians took refuge in ditches, ravines, or any place they could find to defend themselves.

91

As the last few platoons of the cavalry charged the village, Mackenzie ordered his men to dismount and search the huts. The men found bills of sale for Texas cattle, proving that the inhabitants of the villages actually had stolen Texas livestock and sold them south of the border to the Mexicans.

After the search was completed, and the Indians were either rounded up or scattered in the hills behind the village, Mackenzie ordered his men to burn the thatched huts. Destroying their village as well as capturing their women and children would be a significant act of retaliation, Mackenzie believed, for the numerous raids against border citizens whose cattle had been stolen, whose women and children had been scalped, and whose homes had been destroyed. Naturally, he looked at the situation solely from the white man's point of view.

The attack took up the entire morning. When the sun shone directly above them, Mackenzie ordered that the forty women, old men, and children captives be loaded onto mules for the return trip. His men reported nineteen Indians dead, although others probably lay scattered in the gullies and ravines around the village.

This was Mackenzie's second successful full-scale Indian battle since coming to the frontier. Surely this severe defeat for the Kickapoo would cause them to return to their reservation in the United States, where they legally belonged, and would make the Apaches behave better as well. Mackenzie's men had destroyed the Indians' homes and supplies and were taking the Kickapoo women, children, and old men as prisoners along with an old Lipan chief. Mackenzie hoped that this cleared up the border situation.

Of course, his daring raid could not yet be called a complete success. He still had the problem of returning his men safely to American soil. Safe ground rested sixty-three miles away, across strange land, and the Indians or Mexicans could attack anywhere along the route. Mackenzie nervously twitched the stubs of the fingers on his right hand, wanting to finish his business at Remolina, head out with the prisoners, and be on his way before any escaping Indians spread the news of the soldiers' presence in Mexico.

He called for the platoons and their captives to be assembled for the return. He then learned of the casualties among his own men. One trooper lay dead, and two others suffered serious wounds.

At about 1:00 P.M., Mackenzie started his command on its homeward journey. The torrid Mexican sun beat down on them. Mackenzie wanted to return to the American side of the Rio Grande as quickly as possible, because next to the river lay a town called Saragossa, where Mexican ranchers lived. If they heard of the raid, these ranchers surely would be angered by an invasion of their country. They might try to avenge Mackenzie's attack. For this reason the colonel feared to return the way he had come. The abandoned packs would thus have to remain on the earlier trail, while the hungry soldiers plodded home a different way. The men rode slowly because of their Kickapoo and Lipan prisoners and their tired mounts.

Even after the sun had set brilliantly behind the Mexican foothills, Mackenzie and his men were still traveling on Mexican soil. The fear of ambush became greater at night, when each shadow represented a possible hostile threat. Many of the men dozed in their saddles. For some troopers, their second night without sleep loomed ahead. Mackenzie and a few men from Fort Clark had not slept in three nights. The colonel kept his officers riding up and down the column of men, arousing any soldier who fell asleep in the saddle.

At daylight they reached the welcome waters of the Rio Grande, but the narrowness of the crossing at that point demanded that the troopers wade across in single file. After an agonizingly long time in which the men still feared an attack, all of the soldiers rested safely on the Texas side.

Mackenzie immediately ordered his tired command into camp, but he took the precaution of setting up picket lines and sleeping parties for defense. The saddles, which the men finally removed from their horses' backs, had remained in place for nearly fifty hours. Mackenzie and the troopers he had brought from Fort Clark had ridden for over fifty hours. The men had eaten no food for two days, except for the hard bread given to them when the packs had been dropped.

Van Green, one of the scouts, owned a ranch near the fording place on the Rio Grande. He went home and quickly returned with several barrels of a Mexican liquor for the men. But Mackenzie made the officers pour it out on the ground to keep the men from drinking it. He told them that on their empty stomachs and in their nervous and strained condition, it was not the proper stimulant. Many soldiers protested, but Mackenzie knew he held the responsibility for the welfare of his exhausted command, and he acted accordingly. It was for actions like this that Ranald Mackenzie was not always loved by his men — although they did always respect him. His sternness made him an excellent leader of troops, and his men knew it. Mackenzie did not court the approval of his men, but merely sought to do the job the Army had sent him to do.

Immediately after returning to the Texas side of the Rio Grande, Mackenzie sent a courier to his fellow officer, Col. W. R. Shafter, at nearby Fort Duncan. Mackenzie asked for two days' rations and an ambulance for his two wounded soldiers. Colonel Shafter promptly sent the supplies and personally visited Mackenzie, whose command was remaining at Van Green's ranch for a two-day rest.

Mackenzie returned the captured horses to their original owners in Texas and sent the prisoners, mostly Kickapoos, to the Kickapoo reservation in Kansas.

Sometime after the raid, two of Mackenzie's officers, Capt. Eugene B. Beaumont and Capt. N. B. McLaughlin, asked the young colonel if he had possessed any written

94

orders for the crossover into Mexico. Mackenzie told them that he did not. The officers then protested that had they known he held no orders to cross the border, they would not have crossed with him. Mackenzie told them that he would have shot any man who refused to follow orders. Sheridan had granted Mackenzie the authority to do anything he needed to do, even though no specific written orders for the bold raid had actually been issued.

While McLaughlin and Beaumont were belatedly worrying about being attacked on foreign soil, and complaining that their commander had not possessed orders to be there, newspapers mistakenly reported the death of many Fourth Cavalry troopers, including Mackenzie. A story in *The New York Times* reported that Mackenzie had died when the Kickapoos fought to avenge Mackenzie's battle with them. Four days after printing the story, the paper ran a retraction. For the second time in less than a year, newspapers had erroneously reported Mackenzie killed.

The Remolina raid caused repercussions besides the one with Mackenzie's officers. Many reports circulated that his crossing of the border to attack citizens of a peaceful neighbor might instigate hostilities with Mexico. Some people even accused President Grant of wanting a war to cover up the furor over the financial scandals in Washington. Others claimed that the president wanted war to assure his own reelection.

A writer in the *Galveston Daily News* in June insisted that Mackenzie's raid had violated international law: "Put England in Mexico's place, and what would have been the result: The Mason and Slidell affair will serve for an example."

The writer probably had no way of knowing that the Slidell he mentioned in the *Trent* affair with England during the Civil War was Mackenzie's own uncle. The writer meant that even as the Mason-Slidell incident had almost caused a war with England, so Mackenzie's border crossing might now also cause one with Mexico.

Even while Mackenzie led his men in the attack against Remolina, two Indian commissioners from the United State negotiated in Mexico. They attempted to persuade the Kickapoos to return to their original reservation in the United States. That would have been one solution to the problem of their raids across the border. If returned to their proper reservation in Kansas, the Kickapoos could no longer harass the Rio Grande frontier. That would leave only the Lipan Apaches to deal with. Within a few months the Kickapoo tribe, which numbered more than 300, agreed to return to Kansas. Even the commissioners agreed that Mackenzie's raid, and especially the fact that he took many of the Kickapoo women, children and old men as captives, eventually effected the removal of the Indians. At first, as a matter of good faith, the commissioners had wanted to return the prisoners to the Kickapoos while the Indians remained in Mexico. But Mackenzie and his military superiors refused to surrender the prisoners on the grounds that the Kickapoos would be more likely to fulfill their promise to return to the United States if their families remained captives until they came. The commissioners finally agreed with the military thinking. Most of the Kickapoo finally returned to the United States.

For the second time in less than a year, captives taken by Mackenzie in a successful battle became the instrument for bringing rebellious Indians to terms.

Reaction in Texas to Mackenzie's Remolina raid proved overwhelmingly favorable. Most newspapers lauded him; the state legislature even met in joint session to draft a resolution of praise for his action to protect Texas citizens. His superiors — Augur, Sheridan, Belknap — all expressed approval for his bold deed.

Mackenzie kept patrols in the area constantly, and conditions on the southern border greatly improved. Cattle losses declined.

Because of a severe bout with rheumatism, Mackenzie took a long leave in August and went back to the East.

He did not return to Texas until the following February. Five months later, he led some of his Fourth Cavalry troopers across the river in pursuit of cattle thieves, but he turned back when he discovered he was following Mexicans, not Indians. Smaller detachments commanded by some of his officers crossed the border several times.

As a result of these actions, conditions on the southern Texas border became relatively quiet — so quiet, in fact, that Washington military officials decided that Mackenzie's fighting talents could be put to better use elsewhere. Hostilities were erupting again in northern Texas in what appeared to be a full-scale Indian war.

Chapter Fifteen

Indian War!

C olonel Mackenzie looked up from his desk in the officers' quarters at Fort Concho to find entering his door a short, unwashed half-breed dressed in filthy trousers and a buckskin shirt. The man, named Johnson, had heard that Mackenzie was planning another expedition into the Llano Estacado soon and needed to hire a scout. Mackenzie was glad to have another scout who knew the Staked Plains, and he hired Johnson at once.

Ranald continued preparations for his return to the Texas Panhandle and to his dealings with the renegade Comanches and Kiowas from the Fort Sill reservation. He and his troopers of the Fourth Cavalry soon moved northward to take part in rounding-up activities following a full-scale evacuation of the reservation by the two tribes.

All available men from forts along the thousand-mile Texas frontier assembled under Mackenzie in order to form a large command. Even then the entire fighting force, not counting train guards, packers, and others, totaled only 400 men. The garrisons of the forts along the frontier could not be reduced to a level that would be inadequate to protect the citizens around each fort. Therefore, Mackenzie could draw only the men who could be spared.

Numerous incidents had caused the revolt of the Indians in the summer of 1874, making it necessary to organize Mackenzie's field expedition. Any one of the causes alone might or might not have been sufficient reason for the Indians to rebel, pack their belongings and families, and desert the reservation for hideaways on the Staked Plains of Texas. But the combination of many grievances so irritated the reservation Indians in Indian Territory by the spring of 1874 that hostilities became inevitable. These involved the southern tribes.

One very important cause of the outbreak — a cause Mackenzie had spoken about frequently — was that the Indian policy of the government had failed. The well-meaning Quaker agents did not know how to handle their Indian charges. The government did not provide enough supplies to assure Native American contentment on the reservations. Also, both sides continually signed and broke treaties. White men disregarded their agreements not to enter Indian land when crossing hunting grounds in order to build railroads. While building the tracks for the "big iron horses," the workers felled trees used for Indian places of burial and also slaughtered buffalo which were then left to ruin.

Specific incidents also led to the rebellion and abandonment of their reservations. In December 1873, some of Mackenzie's men clashed with a small Kiowa raiding party on the headwaters of the Nueces River. In the skirmish, the soldiers killed the son of Lone Wolf, one of the important war chiefs. Lone Wolf talked war to get revenge for the death of his son, whose bones he carried in a sack on his horse. Also, a young Kwahadi Comanche medicine man named Isatai, or Cloud Walker, called a sun dance and filled the young warriors with war fever during the weeklong ritual.

Kicking Bird, the Kiowa chief whom Mackenzie had sought during the 1871 summer expedition, was now the

99

leading advocate of peace among his tribe. He warned the white authorities that the Kiowas and Comanches had held war dances. Soon after, members of his own tribe poisoned him for his betrayal.

Some Texans felt that the release of Satanta and Big Tree the autumn before had also led to some of the raiding. The tribe felt no responsibility to behave since their chiefs rode free by their side, the Texans said.

White hunters of buffaloes had taken only the hides, had violated a treaty, and had killed the animals on Indian land. This too created a specific incident that angered the Indians. Many of these hunters moved out into the Texas Panhandle and organized their headquarters at a place called Adobe Walls. The Kwahadi Comanche medicine man, Cloud Walker, convinced the Kiowas, Comanches, and a few Arapaho that Adobe Walls should be the first attack site in their war. Late in June 1874, approximately 500 Indians attacked the twenty-eight buffalo hunters there for several days. Surprisingly, only five hunters died, one of them killed accidentally with his own gun. The hunters shot their huge buffalo guns expertly and barricaded themselves in the supply camp, which held enough food and ammunition to withstand the Indians for weeks if necessary. However, when the attackers withdrew after more than a week of sporadic fighting, the hunters packed up and scurried back to Dodge City, Kansas. One of the young buffalo hunters, a nineteen-year-old adventurer named Bat Masterson, later rose to fame in Dodge City as a newspaperman.

This Adobe Walls battle probably could be called the "last straw," for it convinced the United States government that the force of the military would have to be used against the southern tribes. Peaceful methods had failed. Mackenzie, with a growing record of success in military actions, became a major part of that action taken.

General Sherman officially granted permission in July for the military to take over from the Interior Department the management of Indian affairs. The job of

100

the Army became the rounding up of wayward Indians who were illegally off their reservations. The officer at Fort Sill, Lt. Col. J. W. Davidson, ordered to the east side of Cache Creek all those Native Americans who did not wish to be included in the military roundup and consequent punishment. Indian Agent J. M. Haworth, who replaced Lawrie Tatum as agent to the Kiowa, explained the new rules to his charges. Davidson set August 3 as the deadline for Indians to register themselves as friendly if they did not want to be considered at war with the whites. Less than 400 Kiowas, Apaches, and Comanches enrolled by that date.

In the military roundup nearly 2,000 soldiers composed the six commands that marched toward the reservation, herding the renegade Indians ahead of them. Colonels Mackenzie and Nelson A. Miles were the highest ranking officers in the operation. Mackenzie's portion of the roundup consisted of the Staked Plains, the place where several previous expeditions had provided him with specific knowledge of the possible hideouts of the Indians.

Although his base of supply was Fort Griffin, the colonel established a permanent supply camp near the mouth of Blanco Canyon, where they had camped in1871 and 1872. The men began calling it Anderson's Fort because Maj. T. M. Anderson of the Tenth Infantry and his men had guarded it from attack during the campaign.

As Mackenzie prepared to leave Fort Griffin to begin the campaign, newspaper representatives from New York and Chicago approached him with requests to accompany the expedition. He refused to let them go along. Colonel Mackenzie was no seeker of publicity, as were many of his fellow Army officers. (Col. George Armstrong Custer frequently allowed newspapermen along on his campaigns.) Mackenzie had a job to do and could not risk lives unnecessarily. Of course, this often meant that he did not get the credit justly due him for his successful military actions, simply because few people knew of his activities.

Mackenzie arrived at his field camp on the morning of September 19 and spent the next six days moving his command onto the Staked Plains. He was slowed by early fall rains and the accompanying muddy ground. His scouts reported Indian activity in the vicinity.

Mackenzie ordered his second battalion to move out, to go five miles ahead to camp in Tule Canyon, and return the next day to confuse the Indian spies who would be watching. Men in the command slept with their boots on, ready for anything.

The colonel sent out a thirty-one man scouting party early on the morning of September 26. About noon they were attacked by 120 Indians. The scouts fired and retreated until they reached the trail of the large command at sundown. The Indians quickly disappeared when they saw evidence of a large body of soldiers nearby. When the scouts reached camp at 10:00 p.m., they reported killing several Indians without losing any of their own number.

Mackenzie ordered one-third of his command, as well as the scouts, placed on guard that night because he suspected an attack before morning. The Indians came within thirty minutes after the scouts had returned to camp. Parties of from ten to thirty Comanches dashed upon different sides of the camp. They fired, yelled, and tried to stampede the horses, but Mackenzie had earlier made certain that iron stakes, called picket pins, were used for anchoring the animals well. The Indians then took a position on a high ridge that had a dry path running north into Tule Canyon, separating the Indians from the high ground where the command camped. Mackenzie chose the high ground for camping because recent rains had made the lower areas boggy and muddy.

Many of the Indians got down into the path and rode up in the dry gully very close to the camp. The main body of Comanches stayed on high ground west of the command, yelling the few English words they knew to taunt the soldiers.

The Indians continued their sporadic raiding until

after 1:00 A.M. Mackenzie double-checked the guards stationed for the remainder of the night. Then he retired to his tent to try to sleep, although after years of field expeditions, he knew that a restless night of tossing and turning awaited him. He never slept well when he and his men were camped in the field at the mercy of the Indians, and when the safety of a huge command was under his personal responsibility.

He also did not sleep well because ten wagons in charge of wagonmaster James O'Neal arrived during the night with needed forage, food, and ammunition. One company of infantry accompanied it, while three others remained at the supply camp. The men in the wagons escaped attack and didn't even hear any firing. The wagon drivers came noisily into camp, cracking their whips, yelling, and generally making their presence known as they floundered in the mud caused by recent downpours.

On the morning after the night attack, 300 Indians again fired at the command from a ravine to the right near Mackenzie's pickets. When the colonel ordered his men to saddle up and head toward the Comanches, the Indians ran to their ponies, galloped off, and disappeared. Mackenzie then brought his men back to camp for breakfast.

In plain sight of the breakfasting soldiers, the Comanches gathered together in close formation and rode eastward. Mackenzie did not succumb to their trick to divert his attention away from the Indian villages that he was sure lay nearby in the opposite direction. The Comanche camp, and thus their base of supply on the plains, still remained his chief objective. His orders were to break up the Indian camps and drive the hostiles onto the reservations. Engaging a host of braves in battle on the open plain would not accomplish his task nearly so quickly as destroying their base of supply. Also, he would not risk killing so many of his men unnecessarily.

Mackenzie rested his men until 2:00 p.m. and then

103

marched them a few miles in the same direction the Indians had gone, to make them think he had fallen for their trick. Then he set up tents to fool them into believing he planned to stay the night.

Meanwhile, early that morning, Mackenzie had sent out Sgt. John Charlton and two Tonkawas, Johnson and Job. Johnson, the half-breed scout hired at Fort Concho, had said he knew the Llano Estacado well. Mackenzie told them to follow the Indians who had attacked the camp.

The three men followed the trail after breakfast and rode several miles, noticing several other fresh trails that all converged. The country stretched in a level plain as far as the men could see. Then the three scouts came upon Palo Duro Canyon, a huge crevice that broke the plains of northwestern Texas for sixty miles. The Spanish name for it meant "hard wood," because of the type of trees found growing in the canyon. Charlton and Johnson crept on hands and knees to the edge of the canyon while Job remained with the horses.

The walls of the canyon at their vantage point dropped 1,500 feet straight down, and the canyon stretched one-half mile wide. The two men noticed a small stream running through the canyon and saw hundreds of horses, which seemed like tiny specks as they grazed in the open. Indian lodges thickly dotted the banks of the stream as far down the canyon as Charlton could see.

The three men hurried back along the twenty-five miles to their camp to relate the discovery to Mackenzie. As soon as they made their report late that evening, the colonel decided to march all night and attack the renegades from the reservation in the canyon at daybreak.

Chapter Sixteen

Battle of
Palo Duro Canyon

At dusk, after hearing the scouts' report, Colonel Mackenzie ordered his command to saddle up. He left one troop of cavalry and one of infantry to guard the supply wagons. Then he took his main command of about 400 men with him, heading almost due north at a fast pace. After marching all night, they arrived at the brink of Palo Duro Canyon just as the sun rose. To arrive at daybreak was a favorite battle plan of Mackenzie's. He had scheduled the attack at Remolina a year and one-half earlier at dawn also.

Long hours in the saddle proved to be hard on his right thigh, still hurting from injuries received at Blanco Canyon in October 1871. His joints became stiff from remaining in the saddle for so many hours.

Finally, at dawn, scouts reported the canyon just ahead. Mackenzie halted his command and rode cautiously up to the canyon. He peered over the rim of the chasm, which at that point dropped vertically nearly 900 feet. It seemed to be about six miles across. The tepees of five villages stretched for three miles along the bottom of the canyon, beside the crooked Palo Duro Creek. Hundreds of horses grazed along the banks of the stream. Mackenzie led his men nearly a mile along the rim of the canyon before finding a trail by which they could descend. The men rode directly above the Comanche tepees.

Full daylight, which approached sooner than Mackenzie wanted, would make the descent easier but would also multiply the danger of early discovery. As soon as he found the narrow path, Mackenzie turned to his chief of scouts and said, "Mr. Thompson, take your men down and open the fight." The thirty Tonkawa scouts and half-breeds, including Johnson, who had been hired at Fort Concho, were riding in front of Mackenzie's long column of troopers. They dismounted, held their horses' reins behind them, and made their way carefully down a rocky buffalo trail. A footstep in the wrong place would send loose pebbles bouncing noisily down the mountainside.

The troopers followed closely behind the courageous scouts. The men stumbled and slid single-file in front of their horses down the zigzag path. When the first man reached a point two-thirds of the way down the side of the canyon wall, a Comanche sentinel on the soldiers' left noticed them, bounded to his feet, and shook a blanket, arousing his fellows with a shrill war whoop as he moved. The Indian sentinel's echo rang for miles across the wide canyon.

The noisy watchman was the first Indian to die. By the time the exploding blast from the shot that killed him had echoed across the canyon, the Indians below knew of the attack and began yelling wildly. Women and children began crying. Dogs barked, horses neighed, donkeys brayed, and about seventy Indian bucks yelled like angry hyenas.

Mackenzie and his men continued their slow, careful descent of the canyon wall. Each step took them closer to the bottom of the canyon that was filled with angry Kiowas, Comanches, Arapahos, and Cheyennes. Nearly an hour had passed since the echoing cry of the Indian sentinel turned the canyon floor into a bedlam of screaming Indians, blue-coated troopers, and loud reports of repeating rifles with their accompanying smoke.

At the bottom of the rocky trail, Mackenzie directed the men to mount up, form columns, and gallop after the fleeing Indians. The latter quickly abandoned their homes for safer hiding places among the rocks and brush that covered the side of the canyon wall. From there they fired at the soldiers. Other Indians fled on ponies.

Hardly any sunlight reached the fighting men because of the extreme depth of the canyon. Rifle smoke made vision even worse.

A frightened trooper yelled, "How will we ever get out of here?"

Mackenzie happened to hear him and replied confidently, "I got you in, and I will get you out." How confident the colonel actually felt, only he knew.

Mackenzie then charged around, giving orders in the thick of the fighting. He noticed a movement of Indians on top of the bluff at noon and surmised that they intended to block the entrance to the canyon, which the command had used that morning. He ordered Capt. Sebastian Gunther to take Company H, clear the way, and hold it until the command retreated.

The Indians held their ground for a time and fought desperately to allow their women and pack animals to escape by hidden retreats known only to them. Soon, however, they fell back to the head of the canyon because of the persistent firing of the soldiers. When a trooper shot the leader of a herd of Indian ponies, the animals wildly stampeded from one pass to another as the firing continued.

Soon the main body of the Indians retreated in the open, along the banks of the Prairie Dog Fork of the Red River. Some Indians remained behind to cover their retreat. At that point the cavalrymen suffered their greatest casualties when caught in a crossfire between the Indians hidden in the timber on both sides. The soldiers, unfamiliar with the narrow trails up the canyon walls,

107

could not reach the Indians. The distance from the Prairie Dog Fork of the Red River to the pass where the squaws had left the canyon stretched about five miles. By sunset, the bulk of the warriors, in full retreat, reached that point. Mackenzie followed the Indians through the pass and kept on their trail only a short distance.

The colonel turned back because his soldiers had not eaten a meal in twenty-five hours, and the wounded men needed attention. When they reentered the canyon, they found bodies of several Indians. Only two soldiers had died in the fight, although several sustained severe wounds.

Mackenzie ordered his men to search the lodges and to burn them. The soldiers laughed at the two documents they found, signed by Indian Agent J. M. Haworth, which claimed that the possessors of the documents were "good" Indians. "Good" Indians had been given a chance to remain on the reservation back in August. The soldiers forgot the possibility that some Indians might not have understood the instructions or not received them in time. They felt that these renegade reservation Indians had killed or captured hundreds of citizens along the Texas frontier within the previous five years. After searching the lodges, the soldiers burned more than a hundred lodges in the five Indian camps along the Palo Duro Creek.

Colonel Mackenzie ordered his command back to the same pass where they had entered the canyon early that morning. After climbing to the plains above the canyon, Mackenzie assembled his command into a huge, boxlike formation around the captured Indian ponies. This "moving corral" marched more than twenty miles to the camp at Tule Canyon with approximately 1,400 captured Indian ponies. When a horse lagged behind, a soldier shot him, because in its starved condition, the horse would die soon anyway. Mackenzie sent a courier ahead to the camp telling the men to move the supply wagons into a circle, in order to make a corral for the captured horses.

The men reached the campfires of the infantrymen

guarding the wagon train at Tule Canyon a little before 1:00 a.m., September 29. They drove the ponies into the wagon corral, and Mackenzie, by now familiar with horse stampedes caused by Indians, placed a heavy guard on them. He and his men had spent thirty-one hours in the saddle without food. Lt. Henry Lawton, quartermaster of the expedition and a friend of Mackenzie's as well, had kept a warm supper ready for the tired commander. Mackenzie invited Captain Beaumont, Lieutenants Thompson and Dorst, and his scout, Henry Strong, to eat with him. Beaumont and Dorst declined the food, in favor of sleep for their tired bodies.

Colonel Mackenzie ached probably worse than most of his troopers — not from age, for he was only thirty-four, but rather from the ill effects of the seven previous wounds. That night he finally crawled between his blankets, no doubt reviewing in his mind the successful day's work. Of course, much yet remained to finish the job of sending the Indians permanently back to their reservation. The huge horse herd constituted his immediate problem. He remembered the humiliating experience of the horse stampede after the battle at McClellan's Creek, when the Comanches under Quanah Parker regained more than a thousand horses. He was determined that such an eventuality would not happen again. The only way to ensure that the Indians would be completely afoot on the plains at the mercy of the Army was to destroy their horses.

Once his decision was made, Mackenzie fell into an exhausted sleep. The following morning he directed the men to keep 300 of the best horses for the scouts and to replace weak horses in the command. Then he gave orders to shoot the remainder. Some of the men questioned this, but Mackenzie remained adamant. His orders said to render the Indians helpless on the plains so they would have to return to the reservation. How better could he do it than to put them afoot with winter approaching? He knew if he tried to drive the horses back to

109

Fort Griffin, the Indians who escaped from Palo Duro would try to stampede them on the way. Besides, the horses appeared scrawny and half-starved. Most would not survive the winter anyway.

At daylight, scout Henry Strong began roping horses and turning them over to a detail of soldiers who led the animals to a firing line and shot them. By the evening, when the area had become covered with hundreds of the animals' bodies, the soldiers moved farther up the stream and killed the remainder.

Mackenzie and his men stayed in the field another two and one-half months and found a few small parties of Indians. Capt. Frank D. Baldwin, one of his Fourth Cavalry officers, attacked Gray Beard's Camp at McClellan's Creek on November 8. However, the Palo Duro Canyon fight remained the major battle of Mackenzie's fall campaign. Although the commanders of the other five commands in the field skirmished with a few Indians, they failed to deal as crushing a blow to them as Mackenzie and his 400 cavalrymen had done in September at Palo Duro. The Comanches never recovered from their loss. They began surrendering to their reservations, a few families at a time.

General Augur and General Sheridan wanted Mackenzie to establish a permanent fort at McClellan's Creek in the edge of the Staked Plains in December, but they changed their minds and postponed their plans until spring.

By December, winter had fully arrived in the Texas Panhandle. Mackenzie still led his men in search of renegade Indians. During the first week of December a slow rain began, which soon turned to sleet and snow. After leaving the command to search for signs of Indians, the scouts found it difficult to locate the camp again because of the severe weather.

Many of the men in the command wrapped buffalo skins, flesh side out, over their worn shoes. Several horses of the command froze to death. One was found frozen stiff, standing up. Six others were found the next day, frozen with their knees and head and neck on the ground and their hind legs stiffly propped up.

Late in December, Mackenzie's superiors ordered his command broken up and the men returned to the forts along the Texas frontier for the winter. The colonel sent his Indian prisoners temporarily to Forts Concho and Richardson.

Mackenzie took a two-month leave to visit his family and friends in the East during the first part of the year 1875. His orders called for him to report to Fort Sill to become its commander in March. His superiors felt that since he did the most to return the rebellious Indians to their reservations, he would be the best choice for the job of restraining them there. Sheridan abandoned the idea of Mackenzie's establishing a fort at McClellan's Creek in the spring.

The assignment of reservation commander represented a new kind of challenge in Ranald Mackenzie's military career. Could he hold several thousand Indians in check?

Chapter Seventeen

Reservation Commander

hen Mackenzie arrived at Fort Sill in March 1875, the impoverished and starving Indians continued to straggle into the fort admitting defeat. In April, 170 Kwahadi Comanches surrendered with over 700 horses. Even the colonel's great slaughter of Indian ponies the previous September had not completely depleted their supply. Two prominent chiefs, Mow-way and Quanah Parker, still had not surrendered.

Not long after his arrival at Fort Sill, Mackenzie sent for an able young cavalryman, Sgt. John Charlton. Charlton was the man who, with two half-breed scouts, had discovered the Indian hideouts in Palo Duro Canyon and led the command there. The robust Charlton also was the man who shot Chief Satank when the old Kiowa had grabbed a rifle from a soldier on the ride out of Fort Sill in June 1871.

When the tall, young sergeant reported, Mackenzie told him he had a job for him that might prove dangerous. Charlton reminded Mackenzie that his enlistment was nearing its close. The colonel explained the assignment, telling Charlton he did not have to accept if he didn't want to. The sergeant, intrigued by the new challenge, decided to go.

Mackenzie instructed him to take a message to Mow-way in his camp off the reservation. If Mow-way came in and surrendered, he would be made comfortable and taken care of by the government. If he did not come in, Charlton was to tell him that Mackenzie would follow him until he and his band were destroyed.

Sergeant Charlton took a half-breed interpreter and two friendly Comanches with him, leaving Fort Sill on April 24, 1875. As soon as the four men reached Mow-way's camp, Indians took away the men's guns and ammunition and placed them in a guarded tepee. Mow-way assembled his warriors and old men for a three-day pow-wow. During that time the Indians fed their four prisoners well and left them alone. Then, on the third day, Charlton and his friends heard yelling and shouts and wondered if they were to be killed. When Mow-way sent for them, he told Charlton that the Indians voted to accept Mackenzie's terms and to go into the reservation. They all shook hands. Four days later, Charlton brought the entire Indian camp into the reservation with him.

As Mackenzie walked among them, Chief Quanah Parker approached him and asked if he wanted back his gray horse — the one that the Comanches had taken from him four summers before. The chief referred to Mackenzie's prized pacer, which had been lost in the stampede during the field expedition of 1871.

"No, thank you," Mackenzie replied, knowing that the horse would be worthless to him after four years of Indian use.

By orders of General Sheridan, Mackenzie rounded up seventy-four of the Indian instigators of the previous summer's revolt and sent them to prison at Fort Marion, Florida.

With the job of returning the Indians to the reservation completed, Mackenzie determined to change the unsuccessful tactics used by other commanders so that he could maintain the Indians peaceably on their assigned reservations. To do this he put certain rules in force: 1) roll call was to be held every three days — the men were to answer by name, and both men and women were to be counted; 2) if any Indians wanted to leave the reservation for over three days, they had to have a military escort; 3) if an Indian wanted to visit another tribe, he had to obtain a pass from the agent.

In addition, Mackenzie sold the Indian ponies surrendered to the reservation and received $22,000. With part of the money, he obtained sheep from New Mexico for the Indians to raise. He rightly figured that the Indians would be happier if they stayed busy at worthwhile tasks. Unfortunately, they hated mutton and didn't like to make wool into cloth, so most of the animals died for lack of care within a year. Next, the young commander purchased cattle for his Indian charges. These the Indians liked and took care of them.

Mackenzie knew that the Indians would have to be fed sufficiently on the reservation or they would rebel again. In August he wrote General Sherman that the Indian Department had failed to provide enough supplies. He predicted: "Unless these Indians are fed and the obligations of the Indian Department to them fulfilled, we may expect certainly a stampede of the Kiowas and Comanches from the reservation."

The colonel cooperated with the Indian agent to obtain necessary supplies to keep the Indians relatively content on the reservation in Indian Territory. In fact, in his yearly report to the commissioner of Indian affairs, Agent J. M. Haworth said, "I have received many kindnesses from General Mackenzie [calling Mackenzie by his Civil War rank] and his subordinate officers; he has been especially obliging in furnishing me subsistence to issue to my Indians when my supplies have been short."

At Fort Sill, Mackenzie's health became increasingly poor. Perhaps it resulted from the inactivity of not having any field expeditions to keep his mind off his aches and pains, or possibly it was from lack of exercise. His lifelong trait of worrying too much about things didn't help his condition either. Only thirty-five years old, Mackenzie seemed too young to be running out of energy. Part of his ill health resulted from a fall from a wagon in the autumn of 1875, when a horse had started suddenly. Mackenzie had toppled on his head and had become irrational for two or three days.

Adding to his worries was the fact that, in 1876, scandals erupted in Washington concerning the War Department. Anyone who dealt with government contractors knew for a fact that many officials paid high prices for shoddy supplies, often with knowledge of the inferior products. A lot of government money went into private pockets. Mackenzie and Gen. J. J. Reynolds had clashed over the problem as early as 1871. Mackenzie had suspected Reynolds of such shady dealing even then. Conditions finally became so bad in Washington that Secretary of War William Belknap resigned. Newspapers played up the scandals and criticized the War Department at every opportunity.

Ranald Mackenzie certainly was not involved in any of the dishonesty, but he sometimes felt included in the criticism when newspapers blamed the entire Army for what a few officials permitted. His entire life was the Army, and he didn't like to see it attacked.

One especially upsetting blast that came to Mackenzie's attention was a New York newspaper story. It decried the actions of the Fort Sill soldiers toward the Indians: "Fort Sill is a young Sodom, and the garrison is mostly made up of men who neither fear God nor regard men. Perhaps the officers are the most at fault, as they set the example and fail to command the men to do right. The Indians have a great dread of being turned over to the military and always ask about it when they see me."

This article caused a great deal of worry and concern for Mackenzie, who felt that the attack was aimed directly at him as post commander. He wrote the editor of

The New York Times and then sent the *Times* article and his letter to the secretary of war, to be forwarded through the proper channels of his superior officers. Mackenzie said that the newspaperman twisted the facts and wrote an untrue article, attacking the War Department to keep the Indians from being transferred to it. Mackenzie felt that he and his men were being used to degrade the War Department. He asked that an investigation be made to prove the untruths in the article.

Gen. John Pope, Mackenzie's immediate superior, and General Sheridan both forwarded the letter, commenting that they did it out of respect to Mackenzie, not because they saw any truth in the newspaper's accusations. When General Sherman received the letter, he advised that it not be sent to the newspaper, which would print what it wanted to anyway. He did not want one of his officers engaging in a newspaper controversy. He added: "General Mackenzie is too good an officer to be damaged in reputation by anonymous flings. He has kept the Kiowas, Comanches, etc., quiet now a whole year, a thing never accomplished heretofore."

Then, in July 1876, Mackenzie received a telegram that presented him with even more problems. General Sheridan ordered him to take six companies of his Fourth Cavalry to assume command of the Black Hills district and of Fort Robinson, Nebraska, on the Red Cloud Agency. This agency consisted of Red Cloud's band of Northern Cheyennes, who supposedly had submitted to reservation life. General Sheridan wanted Mackenzie to round up the rebelling Sioux and Northern Cheyennes who had been involved in the June 1876 massacre of Gen. George Armstrong Custer's entire command.

Mackenzie remembered the days at West Point when George Custer, his yellow hair flying, had dashed about the Point in escapade after escapade. Mackenzie remembered, too, the many times he saw a more subdued George walking off demerits on the parade ground — demerits for disobeying some rule or another. Mackenzie heard that it was Custer's violation of orders — plus his daring nature, which often prompted him to do bold and risky things — that had caused his defeat at the Little Big Horn. Custer had taken a risk once too often.

In Mackenzie's own greatest risk of his career — the crossing into Mexico to raid the village Remolina — he also could have been completely defeated. He had been lucky, but he had been careful too. He had not divided his command as Custer had done. Some of Mackenzie's men had complained, at the time, that by not dividing the command to approach the Lipan village from the opposite direction, he had allowed many Indians to escape. But Mackenzie chose instead to be cautious because of his responsibility for the lives of his men.

Mackenzie hoped that his luck would keep working for him on his next assignment in the Black Hills.

Part IV

In the West: 1876–1877

Chapter Eighteen

Cheyenne Campaign

The cooler air of the mountains exhilarated Mackenzie's whole body as he and his men left the sweltering heat of Indian Territory behind and headed for a conference with his new commanding officer at Fort Robinson, Nebraska. Gen. George Crook, Mackenzie's immediate superior there, commanded three large expeditions in the Montana, Wyoming, Nebraska, and Dakota areas and primarily held responsibility for rounding up the Northern Cheyenne and Sioux who had defeated General Custer.

Mackenzie led six companies of his Fourth Cavalry into Fort Robinson and immediately went into conference with Crook. An experienced field campaigner, Crook was nearing the age of fifty. He scratched his graying beard as he and his young colonel conferred.

Crook told Mackenzie that the situation resembled the one in Texas two years earlier. Indians who had not yet submitted to reservation life encouraged their agency brothers to leave and join them. Complaining of numerous grievances, many of them certainly justified, the Indians congregated in hideouts after committing hostile actions.

119

The situation possessed one aspect not present in Texas — gold — and many men were willing to go to almost any lengths to obtain the bright, shiny substance.

Crook told Mackenzie of recent rumors that gold had been found in the Black Hills of the Dakotas. Part of the cause of the rumors came from military expeditions, including George Custer's, which had explored the area. Soon thousands of miners cut deep trails into the Black Hills. The Army tried to keep the miners out of the land, which belonged to the Sioux, but didn't try hard enough. They ran a few miners out and let hundreds more stay.

Meanwhile, the government began negotiations to buy the Black Hills from the Sioux. The Indians refused to sell their favored hunting ground, which they called Paha Sapa. They became restless and rebellious at the Army's attempt to take away their land. As a result, the government issued an order that the Sioux in Nebraska, Wyoming, and Montana must move into the reservations. The notice, which had been sent from Washington on December 6, 1875, stated that the Indians must comply by January 31, 1876. Poor communications prevented some Indians from learning of the deadline. On January 31 the Interior Department turned the entire Sioux Nation over to the War Department with plans to crush the hostiles by force.

The Sioux knew of General Custer, whom they called Yellow Hair. In 1868 he had slaughtered Black Kettle's Southern Cheyennes, on the Washita River in Indian Territory, in what the Indians felt was an unjustified attack. Some of the survivors fled north to join their Northern Cheyenne brothers on the Powder River. These Cheyenne allied with the Sioux.

General Sheridan was making plans for a winter campaign, like the successful one in Texas in 1874, to bring the rebelling Cheyennes and Sioux to their reservations in the winter of 1875–1876. But Crook did not have enough men. A band of Sioux under Crazy Horse forced his troops to retire after a bloody battle at the mouth of the Rosebud River, on June 17, 1876. Then the Sioux and Cheyennes annihilated General Custer and his Seventh Cavalry on the Little Big Horn River, on June 25. Custer, at the time of his death, officially remained a colonel like Mackenzie. Both men often were called "General," though, because of the high rank to which they had risen during the Civil War.

Sheridan knew he must bring in other experienced officers such as Mackenzie and Col. Nelson A. Miles, who both had fought successfully in the Kiowa-Comanche War of 1874.

Therefore Mackenzie conferred with General Crook about his specific assignment in the area. Crook explained that one of the Indians causing trouble in northwestern Nebraska was Red Cloud, for whom the government had named an agency just north of the Platte River and then another in northern Nebraska. Red Cloud had at first elected to go to a reservation. The Red Cloud Agency in Nebraska lay one and a half miles east of Fort Robinson, Mackenzie's command post. At the time Mackenzie and his men of the Fourth Cavalry arrived in the area, Red Cloud camped with a group of his people in a village near Chadron Creek, about forty miles from the Indian agency. The agent, Major Howard, ordered the chief to come into the agency and to camp near it, but Red Cloud refused and kept giving excuses. Howard feared that the Indians would join the hostiles, so he wanted them nearer the agency where the military could control them. In view of the large campaign General Crook planned, the military wanted the peaceable Indians brought together near Fort Robinson.

Mackenzie's first assignment thus involved bringing Red Cloud and another Cheyenne named Red Leaf and their camps into the agency. Crook assigned two officers, Maj. Frank North and his brother, Lt. Luther North, to Mackenzie's command because they knew the country well. The North brothers headed a group of about two dozen Pawnee scouts.

Mackenzie and his command left Fort Robinson after dark on October 23, 1876. He took six companies of his Fourth Cavalry and two companies of the Fifth Cavalry. He avoided passing near the Indian agency because he did not want one of the few Cheyennes who remained there to see his force and send a warning to friends in the missing camps.

The colonel cautioned his men not to light matches or talk loudly. They continued their march all night — one of Mackenzie's favorite tactics — in hopes of surprising the Indians.

Toward morning the soldiers reached a point where the trail forked. Mackenzie called for Major North, who was an expert on the area. Major North told him that one trail led to Red Cloud's camp and the other to Red Leaf's. The two men decided to send one troop of the Fourth Cavalry and the two troops of the Fifth with Luther North, and a few Pawnee scouts to Red Leaf's camp. Major Gordon of the Fifth Cavalry commanded them. Mackenzie, Major North, the rest of his scouts, and five troops of the Fourth Cavalry continued on toward Red Cloud's camp, twice the size of Red Leaf's.

Mackenzie's group continued their march and reached Red Cloud's camp before daylight. The camp still slept, and all remained quiet.

Mackenzie ordered the village surrounded. Then at daylight he sent in Major North, who knew the Cheyenne language, to tell the Indians that soldiers encircled them and that they must surrender. Immediately women and children scampered for the brush around the camp to hide themselves, but the soldiers drove them back. The braves remained in camp, but troopers quickly took their weapons away. The attack happened so suddenly that the Cheyenne could not put up much of a fight.

Mackenzie noticed that the guns the Indians tried to use did not work too well. Major North told him that General Crook had ordered them to turn in their guns at the agency several weeks earlier, but they had not complied. He felt that they probably were hiding their best weapons in the hills somewhere.

Mackenzie instructed an officer to tell the Indian women to get ponies from the herd so their camp equipment could be packed. The squaws made no move to dismantle their lodges or pack them on the ponies. Mackenzie told them that he would burn their lodges if they didn't get busy. Still they made no move to start packing their belongings.

Mackenzie gave the order to set fire to some of the huts. When the women actually saw the flames creeping up the sides of two or three lodges, they set rapidly to work, packing their belongings.

The men of the Fourth Cavalry quickly assembled the Indian captives and prepared to move back to the Red Cloud Agency. They met Troop M of the Fourth and the two troops of the Fifth Cavalry under Major Gordon back at the fork in the trail about noon. Major Gordon had captured Red Leaf's camp in much the same way as Mackenzie's group had overpowered Red Cloud. The colonel counted the Indian captives of the morning's work. Warriors numbered 150, not counting the women and children. The soldiers drove about 700 Indian ponies back to camp.

The combined cavalry column continued its march to Fort Robinson and arrived about 11:00 p.m. Absent from the post for more than twenty-five hours, the men had spent most of that time in the saddle. Mackenzie and his command had ridden for more than a hundred miles.

The colonel and his men did not spend all of their time at Fort Robinson leading cavalry expeditions to capture Indian villages. They used ingenuity in devising ways to entertain themselves to relieve the monotony of life at an Army camp. The men in each company of cavalry possessed at least one horse that could run fast, and they always seemed willing to back their favorite with money. Exciting races sometimes developed.

Such a race took place sometime after the men re-

123

turned from capturing Red Cloud's and Red Leaf's villages. Owners of horses from the Fifth Cavalry and the Third Cavalry pitted their animals against each other. The entire camp turned out for the event. Colonel Mackenzie and Major Gordon, as the ranking officers, judged the race. Soon after starting to run, the Third Cavalry horse bolted off the track toward the stables. Mackenzie and Gordon decided that the race would be run later. Even when rescheduled, the Third Cavalry horse repeated her strange behavior, so the other horse won. The owner of the horse that bolted off the course was $200 poorer after the race because of the money he had risked. Mackenzie was sympathetic to such a situation. Once, when he learned that one of his lieutenants owed $500, the colonel gave him the money to pay the debt. He told the man to repay him whenever he could, and wouldn't take an IOU.

Such camp pastimes as horse racing did not last long. Mackenzie knew that General Crook planned another expedition against the Northern Cheyenne and Oglala Sioux in the Montana and Wyoming country. General Crook ordered Mackenzie to join the Powder River expedition at Fort Laramie, Wyoming, late in October. It represented the huge campaign to round up the Indians responsible for the Custer defeat.

Chapter Nineteen

Willow Creek Battle

olonel Mackenzie led one of the largest groups of cavalrymen ever under his command as he rode westward out of Fort Robinson, Nebraska, on November 1, 1876. With fifty-two officers and 1,500 enlisted men serving under him, his big expedition in search of the Oglala Sioux commenced.

After arriving at Fort Laramie, Wyoming, he kept his men there four days for outfitting. Because the weather became colder, the men prepared for field fighting in freezing temperatures. Mackenzie ordered that each soldier be given heavy underclothing, a fur cap, gloves, leggings, and arctic overshoes. Each man also received two blankets. Officers issued tents and assigned four men to each.

Lt. Henry Lawton of the Fourth Cavalry, who had served as Mackenzie's quartermaster in Texas for four years, returned from a tour of recruiting duty in the East in November 1876. Despite Lawton's low rank, the colonel promptly made him quartermaster of mounted troops for the huge command. Mackenzie liked young Lawton's ability to have supplies ready whenever needed. The colonel then placed a major over the entire expedition, as quartermaster. Four hundred pack mules and 168 wagons carried the supplies needed by the large command.

The men marched the 100 miles to Fort Fetterman in five days. Then the colonel moved his men 100 miles farther in five more days to reach the Powder River crossing, called Cantonment Reno, established to protect supplies of military expeditions. Fort Reno, Wyoming, lay twenty-seven miles northeast of the present town of Kaycee. The men faced a biting storm during much of their traveling. The Powder River looked unbearably cold, with ice flowing in it.

While Mackenzie and his entire command remained at Reno, a number of miners from Montana straggled into camp nearly starved, suffering considerably from the blizzard. Mackenzie remained at Reno only long enough to allow the storm to subside. On Wednesday, November 22, he continued his march to Crazy Woman Fork, a branch of the Powder River, about twenty miles away. Following Crook's instructions, he searched for Crazy Horse and his Oglala Sioux.

The next day General Crook sent Mackenzie a change of orders, which resulted after a Cheyenne named Sitting Bear had told General Crook that the Northern Cheyennes had started across the hills to join Crazy Horse. A large village lay encamped in one of the deep canyons of the Big Horn range, near the source of the Crazy Woman Fork. Since Mackenzie's command was traveling alongside that stream, his new orders directed him to discover the location of the village and then surprise and destroy it.

That same night, Mackenzie sent out two Arapaho and two Sioux scouts. He told them to explore the mountains for Indians and to find a route of march for the next day.

At 8:00 the following morning, without hearing from his scouts, Mackenzie left nearly half his men guarding the supplies and led the remainder of his command toward the mountains. Two of the scouts who had spent the night seeking the Indian camp returned to their commander at noon.

They had found the Indian village on a tributary of the Powder River called Willow Creek. The scouts advised that the command not march any more that day, but keep out of sight until dark. Then the scouts would lead Mackenzie and his men to the Native American camp. Mackenzie then moved into a canyon at the foot of the mountains and rested his men until nightfall.

The Indian camp on Willow Creek belonged to Northern Cheyenne Chief Dull Knife. His band consisted of about 400 warriors living in 200 lodges. Following the Custer fight, the weary old chief announced at a council that no member of his band would henceforth pull a trigger in battle unless first attacked. His subchiefs received the announcement in silence. Many of Dull Knife's band harbored a smouldering resentment against the whites. Only one of his warriors, Black Hairy Dog, keeper of the Sacred Medicine Arrows, agreed with Dull Knife that their only chance of survival lay in making peace with the white man. Therefore, bitter dissension wracked the Northern Cheyenne camp on the evening of November 25.

Northern Cheyenne scouts discovered Mackenzie's approaching troops while they were still forty miles away. When Dull Knife learned of the soldiers, he wanted to pull down the lodges at once and flee deeper into the mountains. Young Two Moons warned that many Indians, including the Pawnees, rode with the white soldiers and that a big fight would be certain if they stayed in the valley. Black Hairy Dog urged that everyone move out at once. Lost Bull, chief of the Fox Soldier Society, disagreed with Dull Knife and Black Hairy Dog. He made a fiery speech to the warriors, asking if they were men or old women. He said he would stay and fight the soldiers all by himself if the others turned coward and left. Little Wolf, war chief of the tribe, leapt to his feet with a whoop and suggested an immediate war dance.

The temperature in the snow-covered valley dipped well below zero even before the Indians began their dance. All night long, men and women pranced and sang around the blazing fires to the rhythm of Native American drums, flutes, and rattles.

Late that same night, Mackenzie ordered his men to saddle up. They traveled over rough country all night, often through deep ravines or canyons that were so narrow that only one horse could go through at a time. The 800 men stretched out in single file along much of the trail, but when possible, the troops marched in columns of four. The remainder of his large command guarded supplies in camp.

Just before dawn the men heard in the distance the monotonous beating of Indian drums and then singing, shouting, and war whoops. The Cheyenne continued their war dance.

The command approached the village, located in a large valley. A small opening through which a creek passed constituted the only entrance to the camp. Mackenzie halted his command and called his company commanders to give them their orders for the plan of attack. He instructed Troops H and L of the Fifth Cavalry to charge through the village. He ordered Major North and his Pawnees to move along the left bank of the creek. Then he detailed the rest of the command to march up the right side of the stream.

The route proved difficult for all, but Major North and his Pawnees seemed to have the hardest time. The trail ran along the steep mountainside like a terrace. If a horse missed his footing, both horse and rider would fall two or three hundred feet down the mountainside to their death.

Mackenzie led his men cautiously along the trail. When he emerged on the other side of a small opening in the mountain, he suddenly saw the Indian village nearly a mile away on the open plain. He told the bugler to sound the charge. As the notes rang out loud and clear, the entire command charged at full gallop toward the village. Major North and his scouts still rode on the left bank of the creek.

Within a few hundred yards of the Indian camp, Mackenzie heard one of the Pawnee scouts, who was still on the right side of the river, shout to his friends on the left side. The Pawnee motioned for the scouts to cross over to the right side with the command. Major North led his scouts into the river at the first possible crossing, and about thirty of them became stuck in the thick mud. Animals thrashed; soldiers stopped to assist the scouts. Nearly a half hour elapsed as the men struggled in the muddy creek. Mackenzie fumed that he had lost his chance for a quick attack.

The delay in getting the animals out of the mud allowed some of the Cheyennes in the village to escape from their camp. Mackenzie watched women and children hurrying up among the rocks where they would be safe from charging cavalrymen. The braves remained in camp to fight.

The cavalrymen charged anyway, with the Pawnees and Major North leading the way. The Indians had just gone to bed after dancing all night, so most of them were too exhausted to defend their camp properly. They had relied on the magical powers of a war dance in preference to a good night's sleep.

The Cheyenne men fled up the mountain, retreating slowly after their women and children, fighting from behind every bit of cover.

Mackenzie ordered 1st Lt. John A. McKinney to drive the Indians out of a ravine. Then the colonel watched in horror as McKinney rode into the fray and fell almost immediately from six bullets from as many Indian guns. That young lieutenant, a favorite, possessed a personality like no one else in the command. Four troopers in McKinney's company also dropped. Mackenzie had no intention of losing so many of his men to gain a victory. If any of his men died, he never considered his victory complete.

The remainder of McKinney's troop retreated, breaking through Company H. Bullets riddled the horse of the trumpeter and it fell on top of its rider. The man could only partially disengage himself, for the horse lay on his leg. He managed to turn into a position to open fire on the Indians, however, until fellow troopers rescued him.

The Northern Cheyennes hurried their families up the almost perpendicular mountainside and quickly built low barriers to hold back the soldiers. Some of the warriors attempted to work closer to the soldiers to make their gunfire more effective. A hot exchange continued for several hours without subsiding. The heaviest part of the fighting occurred in the center of the village as Companies H and L continued their charge. The soldiers killed twenty Northern Cheyennes and captured eight there.

Mackenzie rode back and forth from one battle scene to another, giving orders with assurance. At one point he crossed the open plain from the main command to a detachment about 500 yards away. The full fire of the Cheyenne warriors was directed toward him, but luckily he escaped injury.

Soon after crossing the open space, Mackenzie sent for both Maj. Frank North and his younger brother, Lt. Luther North. They also made it across the open space safely. While Mackenzie and the North brothers conferred, they saw two soldiers try to make the same crossing on foot. Cheyenne bullets hit both men; one died.

During the battle a small group of Northern Cheyennes hidden in some rocks fired continually toward a hill where the medical crew busily treated wounded soldiers. Mackenzie asked Major North if he thought it possible to drive the Indians from their hiding place. The major believed that he and his Pawnees could accomplish it. North then blew a call on his whistle, and six scouts and a noncommissioned officer appeared for orders. The scouts stripped off their uniforms and boots and put on Native American clothing, tying handkerchiefs around their heads so that they would not be mistaken for the hostiles. Then they began climbing the steep mountainside.

Mackenzie and Major North remained in a squatting position below to watch proceedings. Soon firing ceased from the rocks where the hostiles hid as the Pawnees succeeded in their mission.

In the valley near where many Cheyennes lay entrenched, a herd of their horses grazed. Mackenzie ordered that some scouts be sent down to attempt the capture of the horses. Four or five Arapaho scouts volunteered to try, but the hostiles drove them back. A few minutes later some of the Shoshoni scouts tried it, only to fail. Four Sioux scouts next took up the challenge, but they fell back also. As soon as anyone started for the horses, the Northern Cheyennes concentrated all of their fire in that direction. The Army scouts made quite a contest of it, each tribe trying to outdo the others and get the horses. When a party of Major North's scouts returned without capturing the horses, the other scouts hooted and jeered at them.

Finally, young Lt. Luther North asked his older brother to let him try alone, but the major did not want him to risk his life unnecessarily. Mackenzie agreed with the major. Major North suggested instead that Luther go with a Pawnee to try to capture the horses. Luther picked only one Pawnee, a half-breed named Pete Headman. Then the colonel and Major North sat tensely to watch this maneuver, which represented the fourth attempt to capture the Northern Cheyenne ponies.

The horses neighed and moved about nervously because of so much activity near them. The creek flowed down past the ridge within a hundred yards of where the horses grazed, and along the stream grew a clump of aspen trees. Mackenzie and Major North watched while the two men hid behind them, as they followed the stream. Each man carried a blanket over his arm and a revolver, having left their rifles behind. They planned to shake the blankets at the horses to try to stampede them.

Mackenzie, North, and the watching scouts heard yelling, apparently Pete and Luther trying to frighten

131

the horses. Soon the animals bounded through the village, across Willow Creek, and behind the butte where Mackenzie, North, and the scouts waited. The Northern Cheyennes had shot frantically and several horses fell, but Pete and Luther came through unhurt.

About noon, snow began to fall, at first slowly, then with greater intensity. The battle soon resolved into a long-range sniping match between soldiers and Indians. Mackenzie asked his Cheyenne-speaking scout, Bill Rowland, to order the Indians to surrender. The Northern Cheyennes shouted back defiantly. Dull Knife alone, mourning that he had already lost three sons in the fighting, said he would make peace. He thanked Mackenzie for not killing women and children. As he repeated his offer to surrender, Little Wolf angrily broke in, denouncing Mackenzie's Indian scouts.

"Go home, you do not belong here!" shouted Little Wolf to the scouts. "We can fight these white men alone, but we can't fight Indians too. Go home!"

By noon the fight began to slow down, partially as a result of the falling snow. Shivering Northern Cheyenne survivors slipped away into the hills, heading for Crazy Horse's camp on distant Beaver Creek. The defeated Indians possessed only a few horses, a dozen buffalo robes, and only a little extra clothing.

The battle finally ended when darkness approached. Not until then could Mackenzie obtain an accurate count of his losses. His officers reported to him that six soldiers had been killed besides Lieutenant McKinney, and seventeen men had been wounded. His men counted about twenty Northern Cheyenne bodies in camp. The soldiers had captured 700 Indian ponies.

Mackenzie sent Major North and his Pawnees to camp in the middle of the Indian village so that the hostiles could not return for supplies. The remainder of the command set up tents nearby, hampered by the falling snow. Indians fired occasionally during the night.

By the following morning the howling snowstorm of

the previous night had almost ended, but the ground was covered with five or six inches of snow. Mackenzie ordered the men to search the village. He sensed that it held much Cheyenne wealth. The men found army weapons in the village belonging to Custer's Seventh Cavalry, thus proving that Dull Knife and his band had participated with the Sioux in the massacre.

The colonel rewarded his Indian scouts by giving them 100 of the captured ponies, allowing them to load the animals with plunder. Then he ordered the men to burn the saddles, buffalo robes, and buffalo meat to prevent the Indians from capturing those supplies to sustain themselves away from the reservation. He hated to waste the goods when his Comanches and Kiowas back at Fort Sill needed them, but only the lack of supplies would assure the surrender of the Northern Cheyenne to the agencies. Mackenzie's reputation for success had been gained by his following orders explicitly. That was the Army way.

Mackenzie realized that he could not capture the Cheyennes who had escaped from the village the day before because they knew the trails, passages, and hideouts in the mountains much better than he did. However, the loss of the horses and supplies would bring them in soon enough. That certainly had been the result in Texas two years earlier, with the Kiowas and Comanches.

Mackenzie prepared to return to General Crook's camp on the Crazy Woman Fork of the Powder River. At noon on the day after the battle, the men began their march back to camp. When Mackenzie viewed Lieutenant McKinney's body at the post, he cried as if he had lost a close family member. Lieutenant McKinney had been young and outspoken and had often gotten into scrapes, but the colonel felt almost responsible for his death because he had ordered McKinney and his men into the ravine where the Cheyenne ambushed them. McKinney had served under Mackenzie since Fort Richardson days back in 1871.

When fighting the Indians, Mackenzie always instructed his men to kill only if necessary. He preferred to catch a camp with the braves away, destroy their supplies, and then capture the women and children. He was no merciless slaughterer, as some accused Custer of being at the battle of the Washita in Indian Territory in 1868. It was rumored that the Northern Cheyennes had been getting even for that battle when they massacred Yellow Hair and his men at the Little Big Horn. When Mackenzie returned from the expedition, Crook praised him highly for his success. The battle at Dull Knife's village on Willow Creek constituted the only real engagement with Indians by any of the soldiers in Crook's entire Powder River campaign that fall. Crook wired the War Department the following message: "I can't commend too highly [Mackenzie's] brilliant achievements and the gallantry of the troops of his command. This will be a terrible blow to the hostiles, as those Cheyennes were not only their bravest warriors but have been the head and front of most all the raids and devilry committed in this country."

At Fort Laramie, Colonel Mackenzie found orders waiting for him to proceed to Washington. President Grant wanted him to command troops there in case the disputed election between Democrat Samuel J. Tilden and Republican Rutherford B. Hayes created a national emergency. Mackenzie remained in the capital until the crisis passed in late February. He returned to Nebraska and the Dakota area by early March of 1877.

Dull Knife and his band of Northern Cheyennes surrendered to Colonel Mackenzie on April 21 at Fort Robinson, after being out all winter. The old chief said, "You are the one I was afraid of when you came here last summer."

Crazy Horse and hundreds of his people surrendered to Mackenzie two weeks later, bringing 2,000 horses with them. Thus the Sioux and Northern Cheyenne war ended for Mackenzie. Other officers remained in the area rounding up scattered hostiles and seeking Sitting Bull and his Sioux.

Mackenzie and his Fourth Cavalry headed back to Fort Sill late in May. He turned 937 destitute Northern Cheyennes over to the Indian agent at Fort Reno, Indian Territory, telling him to see that they were well fed and well treated. Feeding the reservation Indians sufficiently sometimes proved difficult for the Indian agent. Government supplies might have fed the Indians well for six months, but a yearly allotment certainly did not stretch over twelve months. After a year at the agency, half the Northern Cheyennes died of starvation or fever.

In the fall of 1877, Mackenzie received orders to return to Fort Clark on the southern border of Texas. This prevented him from remaining at Fort Sill to help secure adequate food for the defeated Cheyennes as he had done for the Comanches and Kiowas. During Mackenzie's three-year absence from the southern border, hostiles from Mexico had resumed their raids. Mackenzie's superiors in Washington wanted him to correct the situation once again.

Conditions called for Mackenzie's bold action on the Rio Grande border, so he traveled there according to orders. However, his stabilizing influence would have helped if he could have remained in the Indian Territory and Fort Sill. Several months after Mackenzie left there for the Mexican border, Dull Knife, Little Wolf, and 300 of their Northern Cheyennes left the reservation without permission, to return to their homeland in the Black Hills. Few survived the trip.

Part V

Final Years — In the Southwest: 1877–1889

Chapter Twenty

More Border Problems

L ate in the fall of 1877, Mackenzie and troopers of his Fourth Cavalry traveled from Fort Sill to the southern border of Texas. As they passed through the frontier town of Henrietta, located in northern Texas halfway between Fort Sill and Fort Richardson, the townspeople gave a party in their honor.

Mackenzie sat to the side and watched his men dance with the few women present. The colonel, shy with women, usually had to be prodded into inviting a lady to dance. Florida Tunstall, now Mrs. Redford Sharpe, had been one of the few girls with whom he had felt at ease enough to be himself.

Mackenzie remembered other parties, back at Fort Richardson, when young Lt. Robert Carter used to tease Mackenzie about women. But Carter had retired from the service months earlier because of recurring trouble with the leg he had injured at Blanco Canyon in 1871. Mackenzie seemed withdrawn even from his own men at times. Officers his own age held lower rank than he, and he needed to maintain a certain reserve with them as their commander. Men of rank equal to Mackenzie usually were much older, and he could not feel as close to them for that reason.

The colonel's thoughts were interrupted when the party grew louder. Some of the men became a little noisy at the punch bowl. Mackenzie felt reasonably sure that some of his soldiers had added a few "spirits" to the drink. Before the evening ended, he possessed no doubts about the punch. Many of the men in his command had become so tipsy by then that they didn't even notice the near-zero weather as they rode back to their camp outside town.

Mackenzie ordered an officer to find out who had put the liquor in the punch and then to break him to private. The colonel, who was not a drinker, would not tolerate drunkenness in his command. Perhaps some of those unjust criticisms of the Army by the New York newspapers still bothered him. The writers had referred to "drunken soldiers" at Fort Sill.

The following morning Mackenzie led a tired column of soldiers southward toward Jacksboro and Fort Richardson. Many of his men suffered from hangovers. The colonel led the men southward and considered the jogging of the horses sufficient punishment for their overindulgence the night before.

Several days later, after reaching Fort Clark near the southern border, Mackenzie established eight subposts along the river and placed capable cavalrymen in guard of each.

One day in March he conferred with Brig. Gen. A. R. Falcon of the Mexican army. Mackenzie asked his cooperation in controlling the marauders who were crossing the border from Mexico to kill and steal. Falcon regretfully replied that his government did not give him the authority to arrest the raiders. All he could do was forward Mackenzie's request to his superiors, which he agreed to do.

Mackenzie's cavalrymen, scattered in the subposts, failed to subdue the marauding Indians. By May 1878,

Mackenzie realized that he needed to employ more severe methods. Although he knew that he would receive the approval of his commanding officer, Gen. E. O. C. Ord, at Texas headquarters in San Antonio, Mackenzie asked permission for a raid into Mexico. Ord replied quickly in a dispatch: "You have my full support. I advise you that if you cross the river in pursuit of raiders, you take advantage of the fact that you are on Mexican soil and attack the village of Santa Rosa where the Lipan raiders stay."

Mackenzie planned to do just that. He organized his large force into two columns of soldiers. Three battalions of infantry, three batteries of artillery, and two companies of cavalry would guard forty wagons of rations at a supply camp in the field near Santa Rosa. His good-natured friend, Colonel Shafter, would command the supply unit. A second column of troopers, the scouting column consisted of six companies of cavalry and a group of black Seminole scouts. Mackenzie led the scouting column himself. Though still a young man at thirty-seven, field expeditions wearied him because of the aches resulting from his seven wounds. His slender frame had filled out a bit, and now he wore a thick mustache, though his face remained clean-shaven.

A Comanchero guide became ill during the expedition's third day out on Mexican soil. To keep from traveling in the heat of the afternoon, Mackenzie broke camp at 2:00 a.m. on the fourth day. Though ill, the guide directed the command.

He informed Mackenzie that plenty of water existed at Burro Mountain. After marching the men all day, Mackenzie and his soldiers reached Burro Mountain, but they found only enough water for the pack mules and for coffee for the men. The cavalry horses remained thirsty.

The guide assured Mackenzie that he knew of water thirty-five miles away. The men set out across the desert and rode twelve miles before their commander halted his men for a rest. Then Mackenzie noticed Burro Mountain only three or four miles off to the right. The command had traveled in circles! Fearing that his horses would die of thirst, Mackenzie turned his men back toward the Rio Grande and sent a courier to the supply column to meet them there.

The command unexpectedly struck water not far away. With the animals refreshed, Mackenzie decided to remain in Mexico. He sent a second message to that effect to Colonel Shafter of the supply unit.

Within two days, Mackenzie and his men reached the site of their battle just five years earlier at Remolina. Just as they approached the village, one of his advance scouts rode quickly toward him and informed Mackenzie that although no Indians remained in Remolina, a Mexican army had camped in the town.

Mackenzie sent a courier to the commander of the Mexican troops, explaining that he sought Indian raiders.

Col. Pedro Valdez replied by messenger, "I oppose the Indians' cattle stealing, but my orders bade me to repel American invaders."

Mackenzie knew that the Mexican army could not successfully attack his own larger force, so he replied, "I intend to rest my men and horses, and you had better stay on the opposite side of the village."

After sending the message, Mackenzie issued orders for his men to camp for lunch. Then an hour later he sent another message to Valdez, saying, "I intend to set out at 3:00 P.M., and you and your men are in my line of march."

At 3:00 Mackenzie moved forward. He placed Colonel Shafter and the supply column along the right bank of the Remolina River and led the cavalry column along the left side. For several minutes they marched directly toward the waiting Mexican army. Finally, the Mexican commander gave the order to withdraw, and his men pulled back and soon disappeared from sight. Colonel Mackenzie traveled nine more miles down the Remolina River before ordering his men to camp for the night.

The next day, about noontime, a report came up

from the rear of the column that the Mexican soldiers were following cautiously five or six miles behind them. Mackenzie ignored the report and kept marching. By the following day he and his column reached a point less than ten miles from the Rio Grande River, the boundary between Mexico and Texas. The Mexican army still trailed them.

With the American army only ten miles from their own border, the Mexican commander Valdez could not resist one more attempt at having the last word with Mackenzie. He sent a Mexican soldier with a message demanding a public apology and reparations for the violation of Mexican territory by the American cavalrymen. Mackenzie bade the messenger to tell his leader that any apology or reparations would have to come from a higher authority than himself.

Valdez felt that such a rebuff called for retaliation, for in his next message he told Mackenzie, "Guard yourself against attack."

Ranald Mackenzie lined up his men in battle formation and prepared to call Valdez's bluff. This harassment by the Mexican army was bad business. Mackenzie had come to Mexico to fight Indians who were raiding on the Texas frontier, not to engage in battle with peaceful Mexican soldiers. American soldiers had not fought Mexicans in thirty years, and the colonel really didn't want to start again now. One bold action by Mackenzie's father nearly forty years earlier had ruined the elder Mackenzie's Navy career. Still, American soldiers simply could not show cowardice in the face of a silly threat by a foreign force.

"Forward march," he ordered. He led the column toward Valdez.

The torrid Mexican sun beat down unmercifully. The day seemed similar to that May afternoon — nearly five years earlier to the day — when Mackenzie had led his weary troopers back to the Rio Grande after defeating the Kickapoo at Remolina. Only a wisp of a breeze brushed past to remind him that the temperature was not as hot as it would become in August.

As Mackenzie reached a point within 300 yards of the Mexican soldiers, they still had not moved. He continued marching toward them with his large force. Then he heard a yell and realized that Valdez had ordered a retreat. The Mexican soldiers turned their horses and moved away without firing a shot.

Mackenzie previously intended to leave half his command on Mexican soil a little longer, but he crossed his entire command back into Texas as soon as they reached the Rio Grande.

On his raid into Mexico five years earlier, he avoided the Mexicans and succeeded in capturing some Indians. This time his encounter with the Mexicans prevented the success of his expedition against the raiding Indians. At least the Mexicans would know for sure that the United States was determined to have no more raids against its citizens.

Soon after his return to Fort Clark, Mackenzie received a message from General Ord, who was at San Antonio. The message said that President Porfirio Diaz of Mexico protested the invasion but that Ord believed Diaz would try to establish law and order on the border. Diaz wanted to maintain peace with the United States so that he could encourage Americans to invest their capital in industry in his country. For that reason he could not afford to have strained relations with his big neighbor to the north.

General Ord further told Mackenzie to continue his raids across the border, but he placed two restrictions: "Be following a party of marauders and avoid contact with the Mexican soldiers." Several such excursions occurred within the next few weeks.

Within two months the situation along the border improved. Mexican newspapers began blaming their own officials for not keeping law and order and for protesting instead about the American invasion of their territory.

142

The Mexican government established posts along the border and sent word to Colonel Mackenzie that they would cooperate to put an end to the raiding of the Lipan Apache and half-breed thieves.

The colonel remained at Fort Clark another year to maintain peace. One night he strolled out of his quarters at Fort Clark and stood on the rough verandah, gazing up at the stairs. One of his officers walked up and said, grinning, "There's Miles between you and that star, Colonel."

Ranald Mackenzie knew what the man meant. Col. Nelson A. Miles held the same officer's standing as Mackenzie, but because Miles was older, he might receive his brigadier general's star first. Miles had commanded one of the six columns in the Indian War of 1874, when the Army had cleared northern Texas of hostiles and drove them back onto the reservation. However, Mackenzie commanded the only column that had engaged the Indians in a large battle and destroyed their supplies and horse herd. Colonel Miles also had participated in the expedition in Wyoming to round up the rebellious Sioux and Cheyennes and had remained in the northwest to continue Indian campaigning there.

Although thirty-eight would be a very young age for a general, Mackenzie had once served as a brevet major general at age twenty-four, during the Civil War. He wanted his general's star, but he would have to wait until his superiors awarded it.

Even while he stood on the porch at Fort Clark, gazing at the stars, an Indian problem was erupting in the West that would require the abilities of the capable Colonel Mackenzie. His actions there might win a general's star.

143

Chapter Twenty-one

Uncooperative Utes

anald Mackenzie possessed a nervous nature, which made him worry and become tense at the strain of his military responsibilities. That he still performed his duties with force and bravery — as in the confrontation with the Mexican army — was an example of the raw courage within the man. Ironically, his government sent him on more dangerous assignments than it did most of its other colonels, simply because Ranald Mackenzie did not appear hesitant to assume dangerous assignments. He always seemed to have abundant courage to perform his tasks successfully. When the Ute situation in Colorado called for such a man, General Sherman naturally thought of Mackenzie.

Indian Agent Nathan C. Meeker was the main cause of the Ute troubles of 1879, which resulted in Ranald Mackenzie's transfer to Colorado and Utah late that same year. Though extremely interested in the Native Americans, Meeker did not have the patience necessary to make farmers out of the Utes. They began to resist, and a great deal of unrest resulted on the reservation. Meeker even decided to ask for Army protection.

On October 1, 1879, rebelling Utes killed Nathan Meeker, his male employees, and the Army command en route to their agency. They also kidnapped and raped Meeker's wife and his daughter, Josephine. (Both were later rescued.)

Thus stood the Ute situation when Mackenzie's orders arrived at Fort Clark to proceed to Colorado immediately. When he arrived at Fort Garland in southeastern Colorado on October 27, the Utes appeared calmer, having already vented their anger against the agent they disliked. Yet the problem of keeping the Utes useful and happy on their reservation had not been solved. Meeker's method had obviously resulted in disaster.

Indian officials believed that the solution would be to move the Utes from western Colorado to a new reservation in Utah. While debate continued in Washington over the proposal, the secretary of the interior persuaded General Sherman to move 600 soldiers from Fort Garland to the valley of the Uncompahgre River in western Colorado. The Los Pinos Ute Agency was located there. General Sherman detailed Colonel Mackenzie to perform the task of keeping order and moving the Indians.

The spring of 1880 had arrived when Mackenzie reached the valley with four companies of his Fourth Cavalry and seven infantry companies. The presence of so many troops in the area naturally kept the Utes in line. The soldiers did something else that the secretary of the interior had intended — to keep white men from encroaching upon Indian land. As soon as they learned that the Utes would be moved westward to another reservation, white surveyors, land speculators, adventurers, and settlers had crowded the area.

Months of negotiations between Indian commissioners and the Utes dragged by while Mackenzie, a representative of the War Department, remained in the Los Pinos area. Finally, he and his men returned to Fort Garland, and Mackenzie even left Colorado in the fall and winter of 1880–1881 to visit his family in New York.

While in the East, he sought an appointment to brigadier general when he learned of an opening; however, Nelson A. Miles received the appointment instead. Miles indeed had stood between Mackenzie and a general's star. Sheridan helped Mackenzie obtain command of the Department of Arkansas, a newly created post, but the War Department abolished it in May 1881 and the colonel returned to the Los Pinos Agency in Colorado. The Utes again seemed restless.

The Utes claimed that they were tricked into moving and that they did not understand the treaty. Some truth no doubt existed to their claims. They believed in them sufficiently to use delaying tactics all summer. In September the Indian Commission finally admitted that they could not make the Indians move to their new reservation. The Interior Department turned the matter over to the War Department to settle. Ranald Mackenzie represented the War Department in the area.

After receiving the telegram from Washington on September 1, 1881, Mackenzie equipped about ten companies of infantry and cavalry, allotting about 200 rounds of ammunition per man and three days' cooked rations. Then he sent word to the chiefs to come in to his headquarters for a conference the next morning.

In his tent, Mackenzie faced the rebellious Ute leaders, who clearly did not want to move from western Colorado to Utah. He told the chiefs that the matter had been turned over to him for settlement. He knew they had promised to move to Utah, and he wanted to know whether or not they intended to go.

The leading chief, a heavy-set Ute named Colorow, began denouncing the whites for wanting to deprive the Indians of their land. A long, violent speech seemed forthcoming, so Mackenzie stood up, his hat in his hand. "It is not necessary for me to stay here any longer," he said. "You can settle this matter by discussion among yourselves. All I want to know is whether you will go or not. If you will not go of your own accord, I will make you go."

He walked out after delivering his ultimatum and left the angry chiefs debating among themselves.

Mackenzie's entire career had consisted of following orders. On the Indian Commission lay the responsibility for either fair or unfair dealings with the Utes. In their negotiations, the commissioners had failed to persuade the Utes to move to their new reservation. Mackenzie's orders instructed him to escort them there, so he had no choice but to issue the ultimatum. Personal feelings often had to be suppressed, for orders from Washington demanded obedience. Mackenzie had a reputation for success in carrying out a task assigned, and he did not intend to allow a failure to mar that record. Besides, his forceful dealings with Indians usually resulted in the end of hostilities and less bloodshed in the long run.

After a debate lasting several hours, the Ute chiefs sent for Mackenzie. They suggested a compromise. They said that they realized that they must go, but first they wanted to return to their camp several miles away and talk with their old men before they decided for sure when they would move.

Another delaying tactic.

"No," said Mackenzie, sensing more time wasted. "If you have not moved by nine o'clock tomorrow morning, I will be at your camp and make you move."

The following morning Mackenzie arranged his cavalry, infantry, artillery, and signalmen on the mesa above the Uncompahgre River, which stretched north for several miles. He looked through his field glasses and saw the large-stomached Chief Colorow and fifty well-armed Utes in war paint galloping toward him in a brave, final attack. Mackenzie shouted a dozen rapid orders. Seconds later, the mesa top flamed into what seemed like the blazing activity of the entire United States Army. Cannon roared and signal flags waved. Rifles blasted. Soldiers shouted. Cavalry by the hundreds plunged down to the valley.

Colorow reined up with his braves and gazed about

147

in bewilderment at the overwhelming fireworks display. Then his big, shaggy head sank to his breast. With a hopeless gesture, he turned his pony and rode slowly and sadly northwestward to Utah.

The entire Ute nation on horseback and on foot soon began streaming by Mackenzie, who sat watching on the mesa. Nearly 1,500 Ute men, women, and children, 8,000 ponies, and 10,000 sheep and goats moved slowly by as they began their 350-mile journey. The soldiers marched behind the Indians so that they couldn't change their minds.

Mackenzie detailed two troops to remain at the mouth of the Uncompahgre River to hold back the civilians until the Utes at least traveled out of sight of their old home. Finally, the soldiers allowed the whites to rush in to claim the land. Within three days, white men occupied all the rich lands of the Uncompahgre River valley. The white speculators laid out towns, dug irrigation ditches, and set out orchards. The former desert along the Uncompahgre soon became the garden spot of Colorado. White man's civilization transformed the land that once had belonged to the red man.

Mackenzie succeeded in what he later regarded as his greatest accomplishment with the Indians — moving an entire nation of rebellious Utes without the bloodshed of an armed clash. He did not reveal what his actual emotions had been on that day. Army men follow orders.

Chapter Twenty-two

Apaches!

"**R**enegade Apache bands under Geronimo and other chiefs continue to raid in Northern Arizona and New Mexico."

News similar to this was printed on page one of every major newspaper in the nation as Mackenzie remained at his field camp in western Colorado following the completion of the Ute campaign. The Apaches had caused trouble for several years in the area. That summer of 1881, while Mackenzie waited for the Interior Department to complete negotiations with the Utes, he left the Los Pinos Agency on at least one occasion to chase raiding Apaches.

No sooner had the Utes reached their reservation in Utah Territory than a courier found Colonel Mackenzie in the field and told him that the Apaches in Arizona were on the warpath. Gen. O. B. Willcox, commanding the Department of Arizona, could not handle them. Mackenzie's orders said to proceed there immediately with his Fourth Cavalry. Gen. W. T. Sherman placed Mackenzie in charge of the Department of Arizona, which made Willcox and his superior officer, Gen. Irvin

McDowell, mad enough to protest to Secretary of War Robert Lincoln, the martyred president's son. Willcox felt that Mackenzie's assignment in the area insinuated failure on his part — which indeed it did. Secretary of War Lincoln upheld Sherman's appointment of Mackenzie. Sherman knew that Willcox commanded his troops from a distant telegraph office. He wanted the energetic Mackenzie in charge because Mackenzie would handle the trouble personally in the field. Officially, Willcox remained in command of the department, but the field command of troops rested with Mackenzie. The colonel didn't like the arrangement himself because it meant that, while he took the risks and performed the difficult job of field duty, another officer held the position of authority with the rank and pay that went with it. Continuous months in the field began to take toll on Mackenzie's weak body. Barely past forty he had become physically and mentally exhausted from nearly twenty years of such duty. Nevertheless, because Sherman placed confidence in him, Mackenzie was determined to rid the area of Apache raiders.

Mackenzie and six companies of his Fourth Cavalry traveled by train to Fort Wyngate, starting September 5, 1881. His orders said to keep the road open to Fort Apache and to prevent the Navajos from joining the Apaches.

In October, Mackenzie reported that the White Mountain Apaches had surrendered, and Geronimo and his Chiricahuas had gone to Mexico. For the time being, this solved the problem. Trouble broke out again several months later, but by then Mackenzie had been transferred elsewhere.

Following Mackenzie's successful conclusion of his Arizona assignment in less than a month, Sherman transferred him to the command of the Department of New Mexico, where he could at last hold an administrative position rather than a field command.

Mackenzie kept a close hand on the Indian situation in New Mexico, with his own Fourth Cavalry officers in command of field maneuvers. He even sent Col. George Forsyth into Mexico in pursuit of Apaches from Arizona who had raided in New Mexico. He forced runaway Jicarillas, Navajos, and Mescaleros to return to their reservations. Gen. John Pope, Mackenzie's immediate superior, recorded in 1882 in his official report to the secretary of war that Mackenzie should be credited for achieving the relatively peaceful situation in New Mexico.

Still, Mackenzie had not received the promotion to brigadier general, which would guarantee the desk job his health now demanded. Citizens of the New Mexico Territory wanted him to have it because they felt as grateful toward Mackenzie for bringing peace to their land as the Texans did several years earlier. At their Republican convention the New Mexican citizens endorsed Mackenzie's successful activities in their behalf. Gov. L. A. Shelton of New Mexico wrote Secretary of War Lincoln that Mackenzie "is vigilant, able, and just as an officer, and possesses perfect integrity and high character as a man. He has in a superior degree all the elements in a military and administrative officer. During the brief period he has been in command he has won the confidence and gratitude of the people of New Mexico. This promotion would . . . greatly tend to the promotion of efficiency in the Army."

The Texas delegation in the United States Congress praised Mackenzie when the matter of his promotion came up. An officer whom Mackenzie served under for a short time in the Civil War wrote President Chester A. Arthur that Mackenzie was the "best man in the service after Sheridan for a large command in case of trouble." When former President Grant spoke personally to President Arthur in behalf of Mackenzie's promotion to brigadier general, the promotion was assured. Mackenzie received word of it on October 26, 1882. The entire city of Santa Fe, New Mexico, helped him celebrate.

Living with Mackenzie in Santa Fe was his mother, Catherine Mackenzie, and his spinster sister, Harriet.

Only a few weeks after Mackenzie received his promotion, his mother died. Her passing affected his state of mind and depressed him considerably. For several weeks Mackenzie moped and brooded in the Santa Fe quarters he shared with his sister. Nothing seemed to ease his troubled mind. Just when his promotion had come and he could finally stay out of field expeditions long enough to have his mother and sister with him, his mother had died. He had hoped this promotion could make up to his mother for the pain she endured so many years ago during the notoriety of the court-martial of his father. Her life had been filled with much sadness. Mackenzie's younger brother, Alexander, had been killed in 1867 while leading an attack on the island of Formosa as a lieutenant commander in the Navy.

Mackenzie seemed to relive all of his own past sorrows, and nothing anyone said or did brought him out of his depression for several weeks.

Grief, weariness, and recurring pains caused a great deal of ill health for the forty-two-year-old brigadier general in New Mexico. He requested a transfer to New York or Washington, hoping his health would improve with less activity. No appointment or special assignment came, but Mackenzie took a leave from November to February and he and his sister visited relatives in New York. He then returned to New Mexico, where he remained for several months.

In October 1883, Mackenzie received an assignment to head the Department of Texas at Fort Sam Houston in San Antonio. The headquarters where he had received many instructions from superiors in past years would become his own command post.

Mainly because of Ranald Mackenzie's earlier efforts, no Indian problems remained in Texas except for rare raids along the Rio Grande border. Thus, after more than twenty years of grueling field service for his country, Mackenzie was finally given a less rigorous job. He eagerly looked forward to his assignment in Texas. One special reason for his desire to return to San Antonio concerned a young lady he once cared for, Florida, who by 1883 was a widow. Perhaps the forty-three-year-old general, now ready to settle down, might be able to persuade her to marry him — even though the twenty-nine-year-old colonel she once knew had not been successful fourteen years earlier.

Chapter Twenty-three

End of a
Successful Career

Many sights seemed familiar in the city of San Antonio as Brig. Gen. Ranald Slidell Mackenzie, United States Army, rode through its streets on October 30, 1883. Still standing was the shrine of Texas independence — the Alamo. The crumbling shell would be restored to become a favorite tourist attraction years later. The Menger Hotel, famous for its wild game and its chicken and turtle soups, still nestled next to the Alamo. The familiar Spanish atmosphere of many churches and buildings with roses blooming around them told of the city's former culture and civilization, much of which remained a part of the life of the Hispanic citizens who inhabited at least half of the town.

Mackenzie passed several saloons: the Bullhead, on the main Plaza; the Gray Mule; the Green Front; and the Bella Union. He also rode by the Buckhorn, which he remembered as being very popular with cattlemen. New sights also greeted him. The Galveston-Harrisburg and San Antonio Railroad had been constructed a few years earlier, and now there were streetcars drawn by fat little Mexican mules.

154

His route carried him two miles northwest of town, where in 1870 the Army had taken over forty acres on a hill for their Texas headquarters. This, too, seemed familiar. On many occasions he had met there with his superiors, Reynolds, Augur, and Ord, to receive instructions. Now he commanded the entire state of Texas himself. As no significant Indian threat remained on the northwestern frontier, he finally would have time to think of his personal life without having to devote all of his energies to his military duties. He looked with anticipation toward his first meeting with Florida after so many years.

Most familiar, and most pleasant, of San Antonio's sights remained the beauty of thirty-four-year-old Mrs. Florida Tunstall Sharpe. She and the general quickly renewed their earlier acquaintance. During all his years of service, Mackenzie had appeared both shy and indifferent in the presence of women. But now Florida became his almost constant companion. By the latter part of December, the two became engaged and planned to be married within a week. Announcement of their engagement appeared in the *San Antonio Daily Express*. Mackenzie purchased a ranch near the town of Boerne as a future home for himself and his bride.

Suddenly, Ranald began acting strangely. Although he never drank alcohol before, he began to drink heavily. He argued frequently and often seemed irrational to his men. Many only assumed that their post commander was a little stricter and maybe more eccentric than usual, but his closer associates became worried about his health. Fellow officers watched him carefully and made a point of not letting him go off alone.

Upon at least one occasion, however, he managed to elude his friendly guards. The general went into San Antonio and ended up in a brawl at a bar. The owner, thinking he was only dealing with a common drunk, beat up Mackenzie and tied him to a cart outside, unaware that he had mistreated the mentally ill headquarters commander. The police arrived the next morning, recognized the general, and took him back to the post.

Medical officers at Fort Sam Houston in San Antonio decided that Mackenzie was incapable of continuing in command and recommended that he be sent east to an asylum. They knew that the ill general, still in command, would be hard to persuade, so they enlisted the aid of both his sister Harriet, who still lived with him, and General Sheridan in Washington. Sheridan had succeeded Sherman as general of the Army, which meant that Sheridan headed the entire United States Army. The doctors told Mackenzie that Sheridan wanted to confer with him in the capital about the reorganization of the Army. It was a favorite topic of Mackenzie's. The secretary of war even issued orders for Mackenzie to come to Washington.

While Mackenzie and Harriet traveled toward the capital, the secretary issued changed orders transferring them to a train that took them to Bloomingdale Asylum in New York City.

The sudden serious breakdown in Mackenzie's health came after twenty-one years of active service for his country and prevented his obtaining the happiness and peace in career and personal life that he deserved. His weak physical frame, which his family had insisted could not withstand the hardships of a military life, had endured much more than it was meant to bear. Mackenzie's strong will had forced his body to go on for more than twenty years. Even his mind finally rebelled — not at more arduous service, but at the sudden change in his emotional life. A shift from the strains of command to a new peacefulness, which should have made him very happy, instead apparently caused his overwrought mind to fail. Family members also mentioned the sunstroke he suffered at age three and the fall out of the wagon at Fort Sill, which affected his mind for three days afterward.

Doctors informed General Sheridan in February that the general probably would not recover enough to

156

"reliably discharge any of the duties of his office." A retiring board considered his case March 5, 1884. Mackenzie told them: "I think that I am not insane. I think that I have served faithfully as anybody in the Army. I would rather die than go on the retired list. The Army is all I have got to care for — I don't wish to stay here."

The military board agreed with the doctors rather than with the sick general and ruled that he be retired because of illness caused by "wounds received and exposure in the line of duty as an officer in the Army." Mackenzie protested the ruling: "You all know me, and have known me a great many years, and I think it very harsh if I am left out of the Army where my services have always been gallant and honest and faithful, and for a few months' sickness."

Mackenzie remained at the asylum two months. Then he spent several months at his boyhood home at Morristown, New Jersey, with his sister Harriet. He planned a trip to San Antonio the following summer, probably to see Florida, but he was not able to go because his health would not permit the long trip. He and Harriet subsequently went to live with a relative at New Brighton, Staten Island, where he weakened and died on January 19, 1889.

A short obituary notice appeared in *The New York Times* the next day: "Mackenzie — At New Brighton, Staten Island, on the 19th January. Brig-Gen. Ranald Slidell Mackenzie. United States Army, in the 48th year of his age."

Even the *Times* had forgotten the long service he had given to his country in the few short years that had passed since his active campaigning. The twenty-four-word item ignored the accomplishments of Mackenzie's army service. Even so, the obscure notice seemed typical of this man's life. Quiet, devoted to duty, shy of publicity, he received little notice of his accomplishments while alive, even less at his death, and very little remembrance by posterity.

Capt. J. H. Dorst, a one-time staff officer under Mackenzie, praised his former commander highly even though the contemporary newspaper did not. Dorst said: "More than twenty years of active life; always equal to any emergency; always equal to any responsibility; always brilliantly successful; without a single failure, and never surpassed . . . Braver than a lion, yet sensitive and gentle as a woman; uncompromising, determined, and just, kind, generous, and deeply sympathetic with humanity in every walk of life; imperious, impetuous, and dashing, yet modest, diffident; and simple; he was chivalrous, warm, loyal, and pure, without fear and without reproach, with a great mind and a great soul, a grand soldier, a refined gentleman, and an exalted type of that noblest work of God, an honest man. The example of such a life can never be lost in death."

A group of friends and relatives gathered at the beautiful cemetery at West Point to pay their respects to the man who had accomplished as much as any other officer in ending Indian raids in the West and opening up the frontier for settlement. Indeed, he did a great deal more than most. Mackenzie's bold courage and endurance of hardship constituted the factors that enabled him to be a successful military leader during his twenty-one and a half years of service. His weak, nervous body, plagued by seven wounds, finally rebelled against the sleepless night marches, the constant danger, and the responsibility of command. By the time military officials rewarded Mackenzie with his general's star and a less strenuous job, it was too late because the damage to his health had already been done.

For Mackenzie's unselfish contribution of a life of service to his country, his friends laid him to rest in the cemetery at West Point alongside the military greats of the land he gallantly served.

Bibliographic Notes

In researching Ranald Mackenzie's life the author studied government documents such as the annual reports of the commissioner of Indian affairs and of the secretary of war during the years of Mackenzie's cavalry career. At least twenty newspapers of the nineteenth century provided contemporary information as the young colonel's activities stirred the interest of the citizens his cavalrymen protected. The *San Antonio Daily Express* and the *Galveston Daily News,* both Texas newspapers of the 1870s, proved most helpful.

Probably the most valuable books on Mackenzie's life are *On the Border with Mackenzie* by Capt. Robert G. Carter, a young West Point officer who served under Mackenzie in Texas; *Ranald S. Mackenzie on the Texas Frontier* by Dr. Ernest Wallace, a former professor of history at Texas Tech University in Lubbock, located in the Staked Plains area Mackenzie freed of Indian control; and the definitive biography by Michael Pierce of Tarleton State University, *The Most Promising Young Officer.* See also Richard A. Thompson, *Crossing the Border With the 4th Cavalry: Mackenzie's Raid into Mexico — 1873;* Paul Carlson, *Pecos Bill: A Military Biography of William R. Shafter;* and Paul Andrew Hutton, *Phil Sheridan and His Army.* A concise chapter summation of Mackenzie's career is found in J'Nell L. Pate, "Ranald Slidell Mackenzie," in *Soldiers West Biographies of the Frontier Military,* edited by Paul Andrew Hutton. A new biography by Charles Robinson III is entitled *Bad Hand.*

Helpful primary sources used besides Carter's were *War-Path and Bivouac* by John F. Finerty, a correspondent for the *Chicago Times* on Mackenzie's 1876 expedition; *Five Years A Cavalryman* by H. H. McConnell, a young enlisted man who served in Texas in the late 1860s; and a book by Mackenzie's scout from 1871 to 1874, Henry Strong, called *My Frontier Days and Indian Fights on the Plains of Texas.* The memoirs of Ulysses S. Grant, Nelson A. Miles, Philip H. Sheridan, and George Crook all mentioned Mackenzie as a soldier and provided firsthand information.

Mackenzie quite often is ignored in books that deal with battles and events in which he actually participated. However, secondary sources that briefly mention his activities are *Great Western Indian Fights,* edited by B. W. Allred, J. C. Dykes, Frank Goodwyn, and D. Harper Simms; *Indian Fighting Army* by Fairfax Downey; *The Fighting Cheyennes* by George Bird Grinnell; *The Story of the U.S. Cavalry* by John K. Herr and Edward S. Wallace; *Following the Indian Wars* by Oliver Knight; *Fort Griffin on the Texas Frontier* by Carl Coke Rister; *The Indian Wars of the West* by Paul I. Wellman; and *Indian Wars of Texas* by Mildred P. Mayhall. The comprehensive work on the entire period is Robert M. Utley, *Frontier Regulars: The United States Army and the Indian 1866–1891.*

A partially fictionalized book about Mackenzie's Slidell relatives is *The Big Family* by Vina Delmar. Although it devotes several chapters to Alexander Mackenzie, his son Ranald is not mentioned. Also highly fictionalized is *The Mackenzie Raid* by Col. Red Reeder, a novel about Mackenzie's raid into Mexico.

Thanks to Dr. W. C. Nunn, former professor of history at Texas Christian University in Fort Worth, who encouraged and supervised the author during her research on Mackenzie for a master's thesis.

Index

161

Dull Knife, 127, 132, 133–135
E
Eagle Heart, 29, 34
F
Falcon, Brig. General A. R., 138
Fast Bear, 34
Fifth Cavalry, 122–124, 128
Forsyth, Colonel George, 151
Fort Apache, Arizona Territory, 150
Fort Belknap, Texas, 58
Fort Clark, Texas, 52, 70, 84, 86–88, 93–94, 135, 138, 142–143, 145
Fort Concho, Texas, 21–22, 55, 67, 98, 104, 106, 111
Fort Duncan, Texas, 94
Fort Fetterman, Wyoming Territory, 126
Fort Garland, Colorado, 145
Fort Griffin, Texas, 24, 26, 28, 55, 62, 101, 110
Fort Laramie, Wyoming Territory, 125, 134
Fort McKavett, Texas, 17–18, 20–21
Fort Marion, Florida, 113
Fort Reno, Wyoming Territory, 126, 135
Fort Richardson, Texas, 22–23, 24–25, 27, 28, 33, 38, 50, 52, 55, 111, 133, 137–138
Fort Robinson, Nebraska, 116, 119, 121–122, 123, 125, 134
Fort Sam Houston, Texas, 152, 156
Fort Sill, Indian Territory, 25, 27, 28–30, 32, 33, 34, 37, 41, 52, 69, 98, 101, 111–115, 133, 135, 137–138, 156
Fort Sumner, New Mexico Territory, 58
Fort Wyngate, New Mexico Territory, 150

Forty-first Infantry, 15, 17, 57, 85
Fourth Cavalry, 22–23, 26–27, 33, 41, 42, 50, 57, 62, 85–87, 95, 97, 98, 110, 116, 119, 121–123, 125, 135, 137, 145, 149–151
G
Galveston Daily News, 95
Geronimo, 149–150
Gordon, Major ———, 122–124
Grant, General Ulysses S., 11, 13, 17–18, 55–56, 84–85, 95, 151
Gray Beard, 110
Green, Van, 94
Gregg, Pvt. Seander, 44
Gregory, Dr. ———, 48–49
Grierson, Colonel B. H., 30, 37, 38, 40–41
Gunther, Sebastian, 107
H
Haworth, J. M., 101, 108, 114
Hayes, Rutherford B., 134
Headman, Pete, 131–132
Howard, Major ———, 121
Howard's Wells, 52, 66
I
Indian Department, 67, 68, 114
Indian grievances, 99
"Indian Ring," 17
Interior Department, 56, 100, 146, 149
Isatai, 99 (*see* Cloud Walker)
J
Jacksboro, Texas, 22–23, 24, 27, 28, 30, 33, 58, 138
Jackson, General Thomas Jonathan "Stonewall," 10
Jicarillas, 151
Job, ———, 104
Johnson, ———, 98, 104, 106
Jones, ———, 25
John Paul, 3
K
Kaitsenko, 31–32

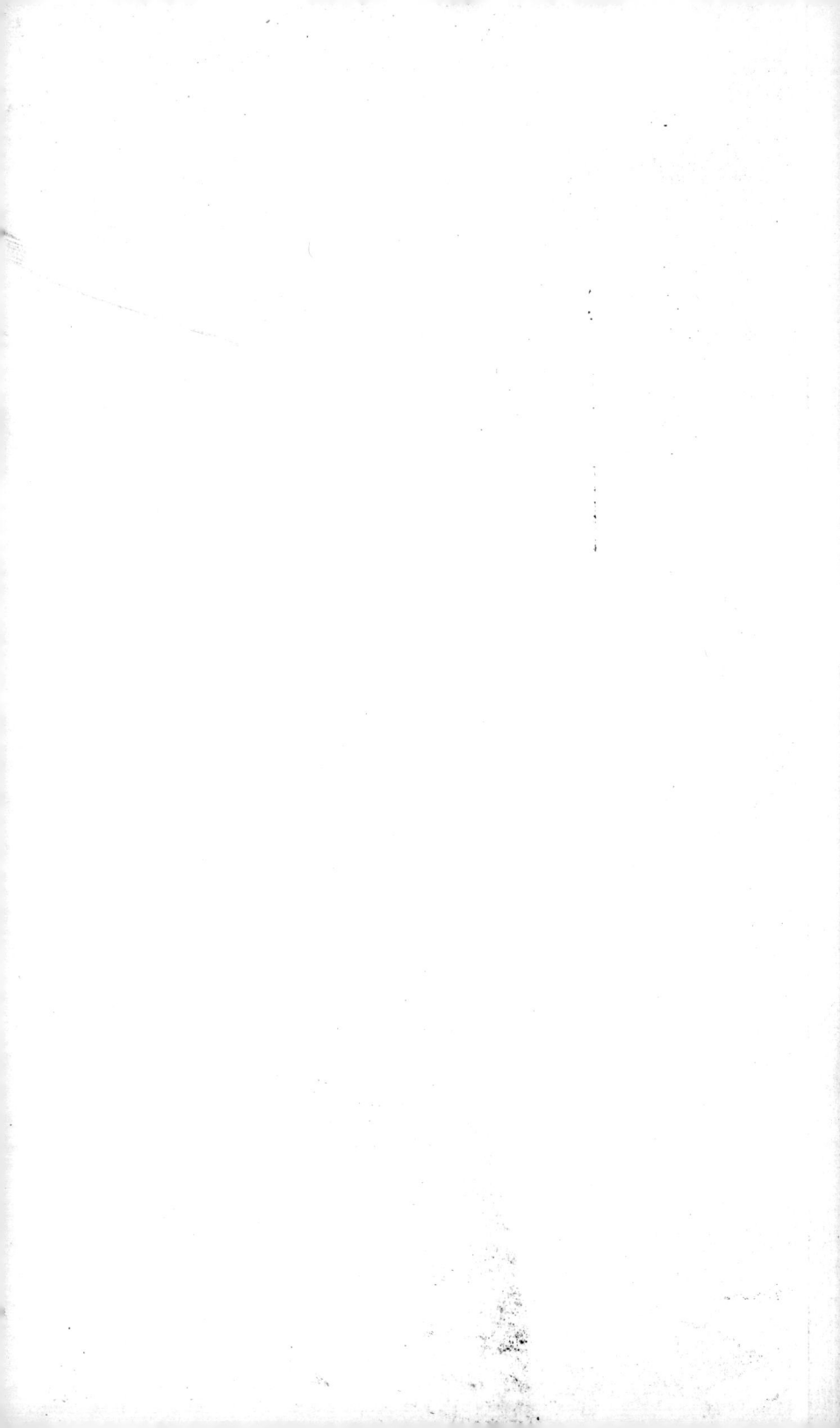